Everything you need to know about collecting bean bag

CHRISTMAS TIGGER

More on Tigger, Page 228

Bean Bag Plush
COLLECTIBLES

By the staff of Beckett Hot Toys magazine

EVERYTHING YOU NEED TO KNOW ABOUT COLLECTING

BEAN BAG PLUSH COLLECTIBLES

by the staff of Beckett Hot Toys magazine.

Copyright©1998 by Dr. James Beckett

All rights reserved under International and
Pan-American Copyright Conventions

Published by:
Beckett Publications
15850 Dallas Parkway
Dallas, TX 75248

ISBN: 1-887432-58-2

BECKETT is a registered trademark of Beckett Publications.

*Everything You Need to Know About Collecting
Bean Bag Plush Collectibles*

is not licensed, authorized or endorsed by Ty Inc.,
Disney or any other toy manufacturer or organization.
The prices in this book are based on the knowledge and
experience of the Price Guide analysts of Beckett Hot Toys
magazine, as well as the contributors to this work.
All values are in U.S. dollars and are for entertainment
and information purposes only.

First Edition: October 1998
Printed in Canada

Corporate Sales and Information (972) 991-6657

BECKETT

Allen County Public Library
900 Webster Street
PO Box 2270
Fort Wayne, IN 46801-2270

Contents

Introduction	6
How to Collect By Kathy Anderson	10
Ty Beanie Babies By Kathy Anderson	22
Ty Plush	132
McDonald's Teenie Beanie Babies	142
Disney Mini Bean Bag Plush By Dustie Meads	148
Other Beanies	244
Market Trends By Kathy Anderson	248

Family comes first for Kathy Anderson, a longtime collector, hobby shop owner, mother of five and professed "bleeding heart." So when she caught herself neglecting one of her offspring recently for what she figured was a more pressing matter, she knew she had a problem.

"I knew I was in trouble the day I woke up and remembered I hadn't seen my Chilly [a Ty polar bear usually nestled on the computer at work]," Anderson said. "Before really even getting ready for work, I go barreling to my store. I didn't even wash my face.

"When I discovered it wasn't there, I searched everywhere. I agonized over that beanie for three weeks. Then one day my 5-year-old daughter is thirsty and asking for some juice, and I'm say-

INTRODUCTION

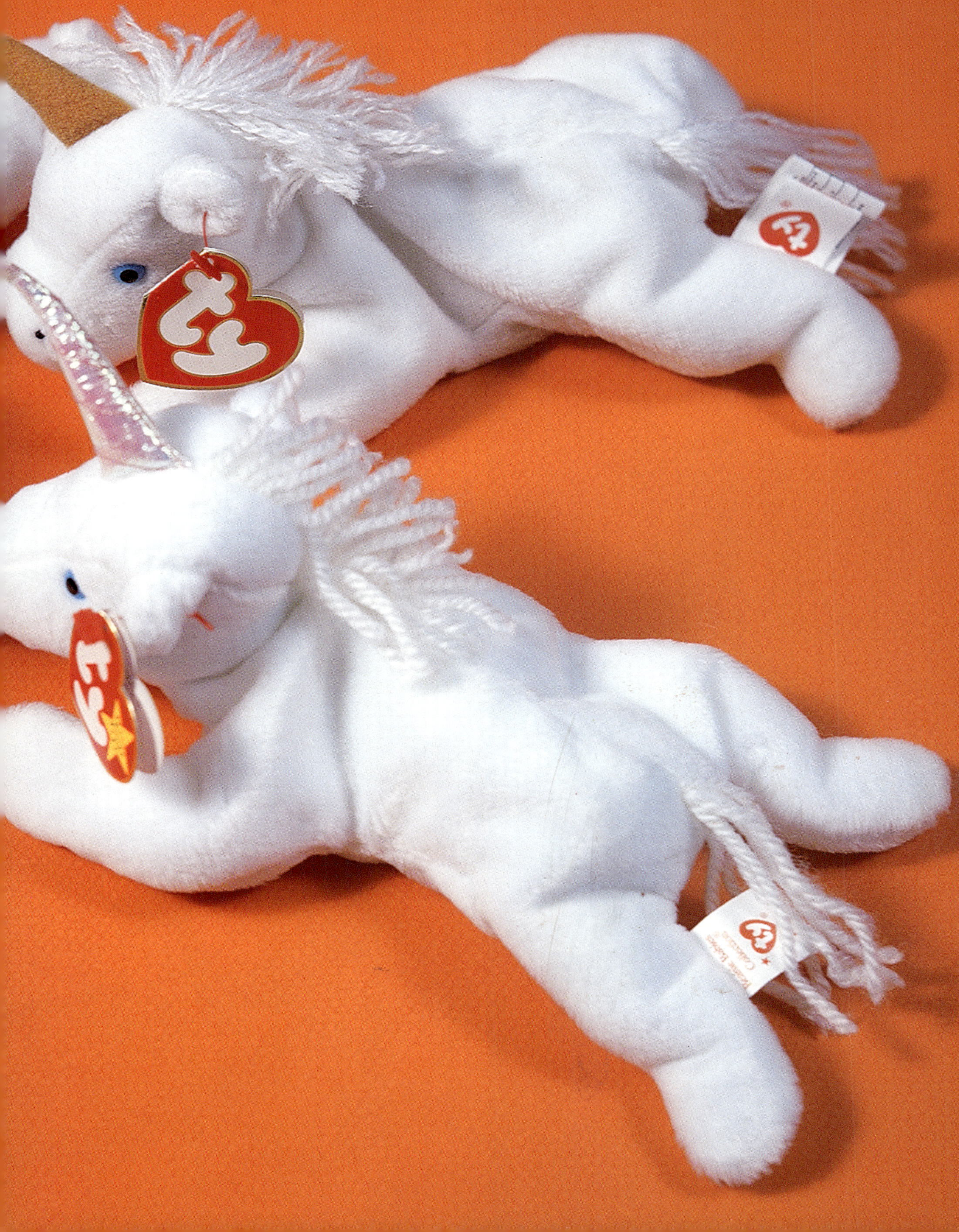

INTRODUCTION

ing 'Wait a minute, I'm looking for my Beanie Baby.'

"Then I said, 'Oh, no! I've got a problem.'"

Perhaps your interest in Ty Beanie Babies, Disney Mini-Bean Bag Plush — or any of the other lovable pellet-filled products on the market — hasn't reached the beanaholic stage just yet. But if you are reading this, you're thinking about taking your interest to another level — whether that's from the beginner to intermediate stages or from the advanced to the dangerous, yet rewarding, level of beanaholic.

With the help of *Beckett Hot Toys* contributors such as Anderson, a 25-year collecting veteran, fellow beanie enthusiast Dustie Meads and the rest of the (*Hot Toys*) staff, we've assembled a comprehensive guide that we hope will answer your questions about everything under the plush sun. Whether you're a dedicated collector or just getting started, the goal of this book is to make your hobby as fun as you want it to be.

The best thing about beanie collecting is that your options are practically limitless. You may want to invest in a particular line of beanies (Ty? Disney? Coca-Cola?), or you may want to specialize in beanies that are new or retired. You may want to purchase beanies as an investment, or you may collect with no intention of ever relinquishing your cherished plush toys.

No matter which way you choose to

INTRODUCTION

collect, we believe you'll find something of value in these pages. You'll find pictures of every Ty Beanie Baby and Disney Beanie, and if you want to know the secondary market value of Sugaree the Grateful Dead Bean Bear, you can find that too. You'll find complete checklists on all Ty plush as well and other notes of interest about the hobby that will allow you to make your own informed decisions.

After all, how you build your collection is totally up to you. And should you soon find yourself obsessing over the search for that pre-Bongo Nana monkey or becoming the first on your block to have that new Glory bear, just remember . . . you're not alone.

"Here's what collectors find themselves doing," Anderson said. "I bought a Humphrey the Camel for my daughter in a hospital gift shop — I only had $10 in my pocket — and then I heard there was a monkey. I love monkeys so I had to have that. And while I was looking for the monkey, I saw a really cool tiger, then a really cool elephant.

"So it comes up from behind and gets you. Even when I received my Ty account, I'd find myself wanting to go shopping in my own store. It's just very, very addictive."

So feel free to follow Anderson's lead and dive into the world of beanie collecting — and just think of us as your ever-present support group.

INTRODUCTION

HOW TO COLLECT

By Kathy Anderson

When people ask me for advice on collecting beanies, I simply tell them to buy what they like.

Why? Because when you buy a product that you like and it loses market value, you don't ever really lose anything.

I was offered $100,000 recently for my entire collection of beanies. I know I'll never receive another offer like that again, but how could I sell something that somebody gave me that holds sentimental value?

To me, the memory of purchasing a certain beanie or the gesture of someone giving me a beanie is more important than their market value. That's

why I turned down the offer — and almost got a divorce!

When it comes time to find the beanies and plush toys that you like, you have many choices: You can buy your beanies at the store (keeping in mind that Ty doesn't sell its Beanie Babies through major retailers and Disney Mini Bean Bag Plush are available only through Disney Stores, catalogs, Club Disney and the Theme Parks); you can purchase your beanies at a hobby show; you can buy your beanies through mail order; or you can purchase plush via the Internet.

My advice is to find a local hobby shop that sells the products you enjoy and stick with it.

Most beanie collectors are not loyal and will jump from store to store looking for the beanies they want. That's not the way to do it. It burns up a lot of gas and uses up a lot of time, and leaves you depending solely on luck. Your best bet is to stick with one store and buy that store's products. Stay loyal to your store and your store will stay loyal to you, helping you find what you need to fill your collection.

If you consistently purchase beanies from your favorite store, you and the retailer likely will develop a positive relationship that can benefit you both. Smart shop owners keep an eye out for their customers' collecting interests.

But that doesn't mean you have to spend a lot of money on this hobby,

either. If you couldn't care less about the thrill of the hunt on the secondary market and rare, hard-to-find beanies, then $10 is all you'll ever need to add to your collection.

"It's a great product at a great price point," Ty public relations and promotions director Lori Tomnitz recently told *Beckett Hot Toys* in a question and answer session about Beanie Babies. "Parents love this product, because it's something that they can buy for their children that won't tax them financially, and something their children can afford with their allowance."

Where to go from here

So you're at home looking at your beanie collection. You're proud of yourself, and rightfully so. The collection looks great.

But you're a little confused, and you're wondering, 'What do I do next? Where do I go from here, and how can I continue to add to my collection?'

Valid questions, all. First, take a step back and analyze your goals, including — most importantly — the size of your beanie budget. What you can afford to spend will dictate which beanies you can add to your collection.

One category to consider, if the wallet agrees, is the pursuit of retired beanies.

Beanies are categorized into two

groups: retired and current. Seems simple enough, but both groups actually feature sub-groups within them. For example, among the retired beanies are sub-groups designated by the year they were retired, such as 1995 (the first year of retirements for Ty's Beanie Babies).

The '95 Beanie Babies group, which includes Chilly, Peking, Humphrey, Slither, all of the old face and new face Teddies (except the new face brown), Trap and Web, used to be known around beanie circles as "older" retireds. But as Ty Inc. began retiring Beanie Babies on a quarterly basis, it became necessary to group the toys by the year or month and year they were retired.

This helped collectors maintain their sanity as they tried to update their checklists.

Although Disney still may be regarded as a baby among the beanie hobby (the company's test line debuted in May 1997), Disney knows how to play the collecting game, too. Seventeen of Disney's bean bag toys already have been retired. Other seasonal characters sell out and are not restocked.

Collectors know that retirement of some beanies leads to the introduction of others, and a new release by Ty or Disney usually triggers another collector rush.

New beanie buyers hope that today's new release could be tomorrow's rare,

INTRODUCTION

16

INTRODUCTION

hard-to-find when manufactures decide to make changes soon after their product hits the market. (For more about the advantages of collecting new beanies, see the Market Trends chapter).

Preserving your investment

Value starts with both the beanie and the hang tag. Many of the early Beanie Baby releases had their tags removed. That's what Ty's instructions called for and there was no secondary market to scream otherwise. Today the tags have evolved into important value indicators.

A lot of people say they take the tags off, let their kids play with the beanies and then reattach the tags. But if a beanie shows wear, it doesn't matter how pristine the tag is. If you're into beanie collecting as an investment, for goodness sakes, buy two of each!

My daughter's Lucky the lady bug has survived being tossed into the ceiling fan many times (The red and black toy makes an interesting visual effect as it whirls to the floor).

I've also discovered that Beanie Babies float in the bathtub and can actually be cleaned with the clothes in the wash. (I found out this important information after Seamore the seal got smacked by some chocolate syrup.)

So if I buy a $5 beanie with no intention of selling it again, I'm not going to buy a $3 case to put it in. On the

other hand, if I own a rare and expensive beanie, I don't want it finding its way into my Maytag.

There are several types of tag protectors available, including ones that clip around the tags and others that slide over them. Disney makes a display bag that hangs on the wall. Many versions of the standard plastic cases also are available.

If you want to tuck your more precious beanies away for prosperity, however, you may want to do so with a ziplock-type baggie. Smoke may find its way into a plastic case or a curio cabinet, but not a good sandwich bag.

Avoiding fakes

All the preservation in the world, however, does no good if you don't have a genuine beanie. With so many people unaware of the subtle differences between a real or fake beanie jumping into the secondary market, counterfeits have become more and more prevalent — especially among the Ty line.

I was e-mailed a picture from China recently, and it showed a massive wall of fake Beanie Babies. So it's important to stick with a source you can trust.

19

INTRODUCTION

I have been ripped off on the Internet, both as a collector and a retailer. And fakes are getting so good, it's getting harder to spot them even at the shows. That doesn't mean that Internet trading or show hopping can't be a rewarding experience. Just be aware of the potential pratfalls. Eventually, you may find yourself trading among a circle of friends, and if you're looking for an especially rare or hard-to-find beanie, there's power in numbers.

The plush alternative

If you like the consistency and marketability of Ty but Beanie Babies really aren't your bag, you may consider collecting the company's other plush toys. Attic Treasures have caught the interest of collectors recently, as well as the Pillow Pals line.

At one point, 10 percent of a retailer's orders from Ty had to be from its plush line. A lot of retailers balked at the time, but now interest in the plush is surging and the toys are flying off the same retailers' shelves.

Ty Warner, after all, really doesn't want you to forget the plush; it's his pride and joy. But whether you collect Dotty the Dalmation or Fi and Do the Dalmutation, remember that having fun is hobby rule No. 1.

Cold, hard business deals are better made on Wall Street, or if my husband had his way, divorce court.

Ty Introduction

By Kathy Anderson

Quality was a major selling point for Ty Warner when he began pedaling his plush toys in 1987, often shuffling from store to store to showcase his line of cats, dogs and bears.

Affordability, however, was his main goal. And although the $10-$20 plush was a quick success in the United States, United Kingdom, Canada and Germany, Warner still wanted a more reasonably priced toy for kids.

Then came Beanie Babies

Warner's cost concept became a reality in 1993 when nine Beanie Babies were designed: Legs the frog, Cubbie the brown bear, Patti the platypus, Spot the dog, Flash the dolphin, Splash the whale, Chocolate the moose, Squealer the pig and Pinchers the lobster. They retailed at $5, not significantly less than they do today.

By early 1996, the Beanie Babies phenomenon was at a fever pitch in the Midwest (Ty Inc. is located in suburban Chicago) where they had originated. Beanies started popping up in gas stations, flea markets and toy shows for almost triple the price.

Retailers were limited to ordering just 36 of each style by mid-year. But Ty Inc. quickly "adjusted" and by Christmas that year, Beanies were again sitting on the shelves. The ordering limit was waved and more people than ever were waiting for the big

retirement announcement of 1997. That's when Ty announced that Lefty, Righty, Libearty (a threesome often referred to as the American Trio) Coral, Sting, Tabasco, Tusk, Chops and Kiwi would be joining the retirement ranks. And it wasn't long before collectors worldwide were hunting for the American Trio and driving their value skyward.

McDonald's then jumped onto the bandwagon with its first Teenie Beanie promotion. The Happy Meal campaign was such a success that the good folks under the Golden Arches ran out of the toys in a matter of days.

Ty's little creatures have enjoyed another banner year in 1998. More publications, like *Beckett Hot Toys* magazine, are donating space to Beanie Babies, and McDonald's followup to its first Beanie Babies campaign proved just as, if not more, successful.

Thousands of Web sites have been devoted to Beanie Babies including Ty's own Web site (www.ty.com) which first was introduced in 1996. The Beanie craze has reached all four corners of the Earth, yet there's still some growth predicted in the Western region of the United States.

Even in his most ambitious planning meetings, Warner could not have predicted the popularity that his creations now enjoy. Despite the immense popularity, Warner is reluctant to take a bow in the public eye. His company is not exactly media friendly, which as we've seen, can work in Ty's advantage.

"I call it 'Mystique Marketing,' " Sherri Shoefstall, a part-time Beanie Baby dealer from Neaderland, Texas, told *Beckett Hot Toys*.

"[Ty Inc] has no communication with the public or their retailers. But that's 'Mystique Marketing.' They want to keep people guessing about what's next or why they did this beanie this way, or that one that way. That's part of their marketing plan."

Even if Warner isn't talking, at least he is listening. Initially, retirements were announced twice a year. Now, as the beanies enter their fifth year, Ty has committed to retiring four times per year.

"The retirements are key," says Bruce Minor, co-owner of T.J. Enterprises in Hamilton, Ohio, who caters to collectors looking for current releases or the retired Beanies. "The retirements give the whole industry a healthy kick."

But at a price, and usually a high one. The vast amount of retired Beanie Babies is beginning to draw a financial line between young collectors and the adults entering the Beanie hobby. Quite simply, kids can't afford the higher secondary prices attached to the retired Beanies.

NEW BEANIE BABIES

Ants the anteater

Early the robin

The New Ty Beanie Babies

Ty announced the addition of 14 cuddly new members to the Beanie Baby family in May 1998.

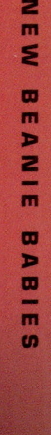

NEW BEANIE BABIES

Fetch the golden retriever

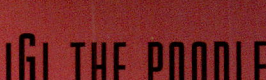

GiGi the poodle

Glory the bear

Fortune the panda

NEW BEANIE BABIES

28

Jabber the parrot

Jake the mallard duck

Kuku the cockatoo

Rocket the blue jay

NEW BEANIE BABIES

STINGER THE SCORPION

TRACKER THE BASSET HOUND

WISE THE OWL

WHISPER THE DEER

1997 Teddy

Born Dec. 25, 1996.

Released October 1997.

Retired January 1998.

Description This jolly holiday bear was produced for only three months during the winter holiday season of 1997.

Availability 1997 Teddy is moderately hard to find, even when sleigh bells aren't ringing.

Value History Still relatively inexpensive and stable.

Ally the Alligator

Born March 14, 1994.

Released 1994.

Retired October 1997.

Description Ally, one of Ty's original nine, can be found with four generations of tags. The first Allys appear softer and more plump than their descendants.

Availability Ally has never been easy to find.

Value History Increasing.

Ants the Anteater

Born Nov. 7, 1997.

Released May 1998.

Description This gray beast with black and white stripes shows potential and is one of Ty's latest releases.

Availability Ants is hard to find, at least for now.

Value History Fetched a higher price starting out but should return to retail price soon.

Batty the Bat

Born Oct. 29, 1996.
Released January 1997.
Description Thanks to Batty's velcro wings, this flying mammal can cling to most anything.
Availability Batty can sometimes be elusive.
Value History Unchanged.

Baldy the Eagle

- **Born** Feb. 17, 1996.
- **Released** 1997.
- **Retired** May 1997.
- **Description** Baldy is a fitting tribute to a national symbol. This very detailed eagle was produced for just one year.
- **Availability** Baldy's short production has made him always difficult to come by.
- **Value History** Unchanged.

Bernie the St. Bernard

- **Born** Oct. 3, 1996.
- **Released** January 1997.
- **Description** This tri-colored canine has perky ears and loves to play catch.
- **Availability** Bernie can be found easily.
- **Value History** Unchanged.

Blackie the Black Bear

Born July 15, 1994.

Released 1994.

Description Blackie is one of four bears that lay flat, and he loves to lie around with his pal, Cubbie. But pick him up soon because he might follow Cubbie into retirement.

Availability Finding Blackie requires some searching.

Value History Unchanged.

Blizzard the White Tiger

Born Dec. 12, 1996.

Released May 1997.

Retired May 1998.

Description With Blizzard's retirement, tigers became extinct in the Beanie Baby world. Stores never seem to get a large enough shipment of this black and white beauty.

Availability This tiger is usually in hiding.

Value History Increasing.

Bessie the Cow

Born	June 27, 1995.
Released	1995.
Retired	October 1997.
Description	It seemed no one wanted this plain brown and white cow when first released. But now that she's retired, she's in big demand and is the favorite between the two cows. Grab her while you can.
Availability	Hard to find.
Value History	Increasing — $75 and up.

Bones the Dog

Born	Jan. 18, 1994.
Released	1995.
Retired	May 1998.
Description	Bones might look like an ordinary mutt, but he is distinguished as being one of the original nine Beanie Babies produced. He's complemented by a matching Teenie Beanie and a Pillow Pal named Woof.
Availability	Bones is hard to find.
Value History	Increasing.

Bongo the Monkey

Born Aug. 17, 1995.

Released 1995.

Description Bongo was first released under the name Nana but was soon renamed. He has been released both with a dark tail and a tan tail, and the dark-tailed Bongo is rare. Bongo's Teenie Beanie counterpart was the No. 2 release in the 1998 McDonald's Teenie Beanie promotion. He also has a Pillow Pal named Swinger.

Availability The tan-tailed Bongo is easy to find.

Value History Unchanged.

Britannia the Bear

Born Dec. 15, 1997.

Released January 1998.

Description This sweet lass wears a British flag on her chest, and she rarely makes it out of her native land of England. Some more persistent collectors have tried to get past customs to bring Britannia to the United States, and she has been confiscated many times.

Availability Extremely hard to find, except in England.

Value History Expensive, but stable. Could cost as much as $600.

TY SECTION

BRUNO THE TERRIER

Born Sept. 9, 1997.
Released January 1997.
Description Bruno's no brute, but he does appear to be the least favorite of the January 1997 releases.
Availability Plentiful.
Value History Unchanged.

BUBBLES THE FISH

Born July 2, 1995.
Released 1995.
Retired May 1997.
Description This black-and-yellow fish seems to have no specific species.
Availability Bubbles makes himself scarce.
Value History Still expensive, but decreasing. Usually from $125 to $200.

Bronty the Brontosaurus

Born	Date unknown.
Released	1995.
Retired	January 1996.
Description	Although 100,000 of this murky blue dinosaur were produced, Bronty is still the rarest of the three dinosaurs. He was first issued without a poem on his tag.
Availability	Increasingly hard to find.
Value History	Pricey and getting more expensive every day. Can cost as much as $1,350.

Bumble the Bee

Born Date unknown.
Released 1995.
Retired January 1996.
Description The buzz about this bee is that he was produced with both third generation and fourth generation tags. The fourth generation is more rare.
Availability Bumble is hard to find with either tag, but the third generation tag is somewhat more plentiful.
Value History Runs about $500 to $800, but his price is decreasing.

Bucky the Beaver

Born June 8, 1995.

Released 1996.

Retired January 1998.

Description Big-toothed Bucky wasn't very popular until he retired. Now he spends his time with the "in" crowd.

Availability Now that he's retired, he's an unusual find.

Value History Still reasonable but increasing due to retirement.

Caw the Crow

Born Date unknown.

Released 1995.

Retired January 1996.

Description This black-and-gold crow is more popular with boys. He was produced with a third generation gift tag featuring "To" and "From" blanks.

Availability This bird is hard to bring down.

Value History Hasn't spurred much interest lately, but his value could rise from the current $600-$900.

Chocolate the Moose

Born April 27, 1993.

Released 1994.

Description Chocolate is a children's favorite with his big, orange antlers. He was one of the original nine Beanies, and he has a matching McDonald's Teenie Beanie.

Availability This moose is in most places.

Value History Unchanged.

Chilly the Polar Bear

Born Date unknown

Released 1994.

Retired 1995.

Description Perhaps Chilly's pristine white coat makes him so difficult to come by in mint condition. He was available for only one year, and whoever bought him for the original price was lucky.

Availability Extremely hard to find in mint condition.

Value History Slightly decreasing, but still very valuable. Up to $2,500.

Chip the Calico Cat

Born Jan. 26, 1996.

Released May 1997.

Description Chip is the cat's meow. He's one of the most popular of all the cats with his cheerful mix of colors.

Availability Usually easy, but stores never seem to stock enough.

Value History Unchanged.

TY SECTION

CHOPS THE LAMB

Born May 3, 1996.
Released 1996.
Retired January 1997.
Description Chops production was short-lived — just six months — making him rather rare. Rumor has it that his production was stopped due to his resemblance to another famous lamb. Nevertheless, if Chops follows you home, keep him.
Availability Difficult to find; grab him when you can.
Value History Decreasing, but still very valuable.

CONGO THE GORILLA

Born Nov. 9, 1996.
Released Mid-1996.
Description Congo is one of only two Beanie primates, and he's popular among collectors looking for the jungle motif.
Availability Easy to find except for the special release with the Toy Fair tag.
Value History Inexpensive normally; Toy Fair edition more pricey.

Claude the Crab

Born	Sept. 3, 1996.
Released	May 1997.
Description	Those who missed the opportunity to own Claude's cousin, Digger, welcome this colorful version. He is tie-dyed in blues, golds and greens. But his belly is pure white.
Availability	Claude sometimes hides in the sand.
Value History	Still a good price but on the rise.

TY SECTION

Crunch the Shark

Born Jan. 13, 1996.
Released January 1997.
Description Maybe it's this shark's ferocious look that makes him one of the least desirable Beanies. But he won't bite.
Availability Crunch is just about everywhere.
Value History Unchanged.

Coral the Fish

Born March 2, 1995.

Released 1995.

Retired January 1997.

Description Tie-dyed Coral was the first of the three Beanie fish to be retired, making him more sought after.

Availability Keep your hook in the water, but bites are few.

Value History Over $100 now and climbing.

Cubbie the Bear

Born November 14, 1993.

Released 1994.

Retired January 1998.

Description This bear made his debut as Brownie and was one of the original nine Beanies. In 1997, the Chicago Cubs handed out Cubbies and commemorative cards to fans. Collectors poured into Wrigley Field to receive the bear. Since then, other teams have jumped on the bandwagon.

Availability Harder to find now that he's retired.

Value History Increasing.

Curly the Napped Bear

Born April 12, 1996.

Released Mid-1996.

Description Curly was the first Beanie to be made with napped fur. He has the Ty classic close-set button eyes and oval button nose.

Availability Sometimes difficult to find.

Value History Priced decently and stable.

Daisy the Cow

Born May 10, 1994.

Released 1994.

Description Daisy, unlike Bessie, stretches out for a rest. Cow lovers adore her black and white design. She is the only Beanie whose tag was totally changed to honor Harry Caray, a famous baseball broadcaster known for his work with the Chicago Cubs.

Availability Daisy is almost as common as milk.

Value History Unchanged.

Derby the Horse

Born Sept. 16, 1995.

Released 1995.

Description Derby was first released with a fine mane and tail that later was changed to a coarser yarn. In January 1998, the fifth generation Derby had a star on his forehead.

Availability The fine-maned Derby is difficult to find, but he is otherwise readily available.

Value History Unchanged.

Doby the Doberman

Born Oct. 9, 1996.

Released January 1997.

Description Doby started off slow until collectors noticed his sweet face. He's a good representative of his breed, and he has a matching Teenie Beanie.

Availability Doby is no rare breed.

Value History Unchanged.

DIGGER THE CRAB

Born Aug. 23, 1995.

Released 1995.

Retired May 1997.

Description Bright red Digger was first produced in orange. His original production number was low, making him a tough crab to dig up.

Availability In red, Digger can be seen about. But he's hard to glimpse in orange.

Value History Orange Digger's price has jumped to $800 but is mostly stable. Red Digger is considerably cheaper.

DOTTY THE DALMATIAN

Born Oct. 17, 1996.

Released May 1997.

Description Dotty replaced Sparky after his retirement. The most noticeable difference between the two is Dotty's black ears and tail. She has a matching Pillow Pal named Spotty.

Availability Dalmatians seem to be more plentiful these days, and Dotty is no exception.

Value History Unchanged.

EARLY THE ROBIN

Born Feb. 20, 1997.
Released May 1998.
Description This tie-dyed bird features the same material as Pounce the Cat.
Availability Even though Early is a new release, she's extremely rare.
Value History Unchanged.

ECHO THE DOLPHIN

Born Dec. 21, 1996.
Released 1997.
Retired May 1998.
Description This gray and white dolphin was first released with Waves the whale tags. These mistagged ocean dwellers fetch a higher price on the secondary market. Echo's matching Pillow Pal is named Glide.
Availability Echos with correct tags are moderately available, much more so than mistagged Echos.
Value History Inexpensive and stable.

Ears the Bunny

Born April 18, 1995.

Released 1996.

Retired May 1998.

Description This brown, long-eared rabbit is one of four rabbits in the Beanie line. The other three, Hippity, Hoppity and Floppity, are designed to sit up. All four have hopped into retirement.

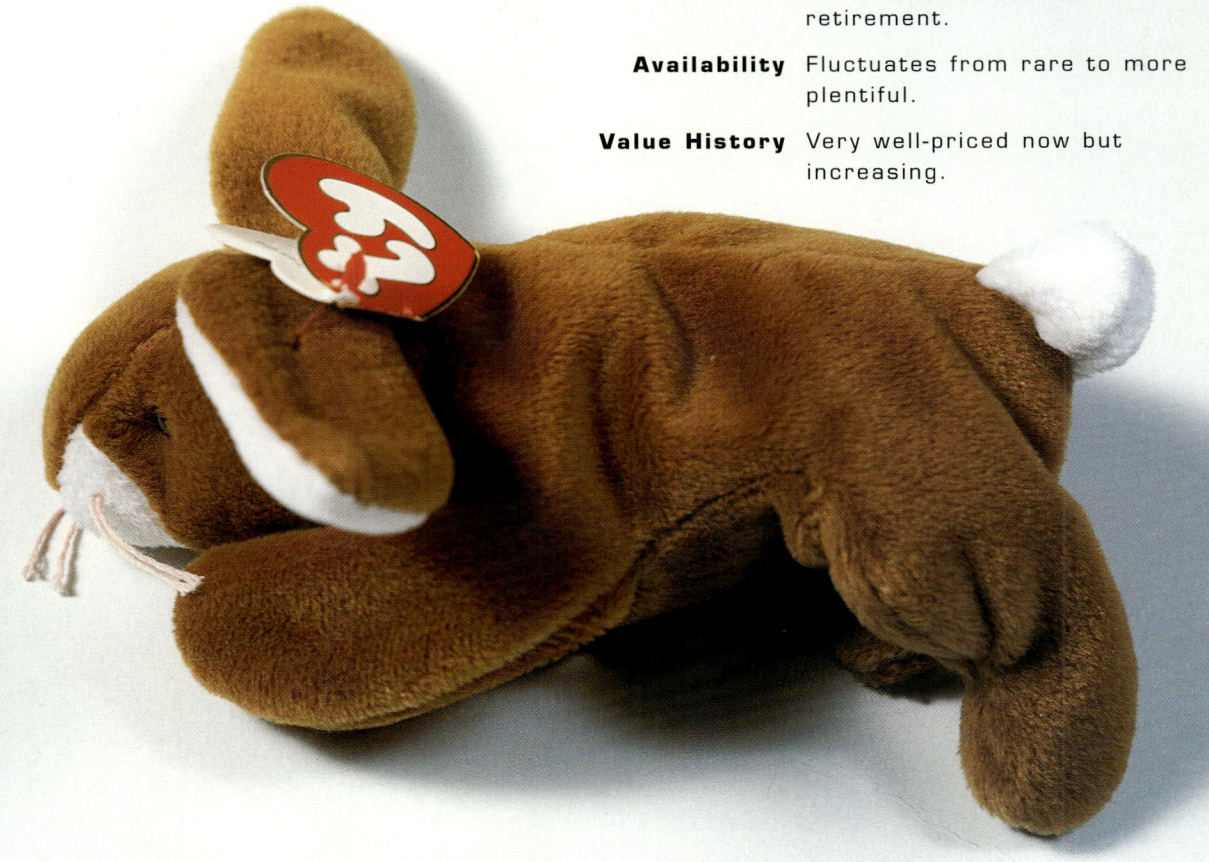

Availability Fluctuates from rare to more plentiful.

Value History Very well-priced now but increasing.

TY SECTION

Erin the Bear

Born March 17, 1997.

Released 1998.

Description Erin, with her emerald green fur and white clover stitched on her chest, is named after the Emerald Isle. Erin hit the secondary market selling for more than the Princess Bear.

Availability Erin is slow to appear on shelves, and you might have to draw for a chance to purchase. Look for her to be more available on St. Patrick's Day.

Value History Up to $160 but decreasing.

Flash the Dolphin

Born May 13, 1993.

Released 1994.

Retired May 1997.

Description Although 3 million were made, many collectors missed the chance to pick Flash up. He was one of the original nine Beanies, and extremely few Flashes were issued with his name misspelled as Fiash on his tag. He has a matching Pillow Pal named Tide.

Availability You'll have to look hard for him, but Flash is still available at Beanie shows across the United States.

Value History Expensive but decreasing.

Fetch the Golden Retriever

Born Feb. 4, 1997.

Released May 1998.

Description Dye this dog black and you might end up with a black Labrador. Dog lovers sit up and beg for this cuddly puppy. He is among the list of favorites of children and adult collectors alike.

Availability Fluctuates, but his popularity can sometimes make him scarce.

Value History Unchanged.

Fleece the Lamb

Born March 21, 1996.

Released January 1997.

Description This sweet lamb with a napped coat replaced Chops the Lamb. He was produced with fourth and fifth generation tags, and he made a cameo appearance on Mariah Carey's video for "Stay Awhile." He has a matching Pillow Pal named Ba-Ba.

Availability Not always easy to find, but still plentiful.

Value History Unchanged.

Flip the Cat

Born Feb. 28, 1995.

Released 1996.

Retired October 1997.

Description Even before his retirement, the all-white Flip was a rare treasure. He is the most popular of the Beanie cats, and he is difficult to find in mint condition. Keep Flip in a container to protect his fur.

Availability Catch Flip when you can. He's hard to pin down.

Value History His retired value started high, but his price has become a little more reasonable.

Floppity the Bunny

Born May 28, 1996.

Released January 1997.

Retired May 1998.

Description This lilac-colored rabbit is one of the three pastel Beanie bunnies. She was produced for only one year.

Availability Sometimes hard to find, but all the bunnies become more visible at Easter.

Value History Fluctuates; increasing.

TY SECTION

Flutter the Butterfly

Born Date unknown.
Released 1995.
Retired January 1996.
Description Flutter's black plush body is complemented by her tie-dyed wings. She was not very popular when she was first introduced, but now she's a rare sight.
Availability If you get her in your net, keep her. You might not get the chance again.
Value History Expensive but stable.

Fortune the Panda

Born Dec. 6, 1997.
Released May 1998.
Description Fortune is one of 14 newly released bears. Although he has black patches across his eyes and sports a bright red bow, he is patterned the same as the other current bears. If you didn't get a chance to own Peaking the Panda, this bear is truly good Fortune for you.
Availability Fortune is shy. He rarely makes himself seen.
Value History Moderately priced.

Freckles the Leopard

Born June 3, 1996.

Released Mid-1996.

Description Despite the leopard's knack for concealment, it's hard to lose this cat in a crowd. Look for the speckled material that is faded or fuzzy. Freckles has a matching Pillow Pal named Speckles.

Availability Easy to spot.

Value History Unchanged.

Garcia the Bear

Born Aug. 1, 1995.

Released 1995.

Retired May 1997.

Description This tie-dyed bear underwent a design change at the request of Jerry Garcia's family. His colors range from muted rainbows to vibrant splashes.

Availability Highly sought after and hard to find.

Value History A little expensive, but stable.

GiGi the Poodle

Born March 7, 1997.

Released May 1998.

Description The newly released GiGi somewhat resembles her friend Scottie with her napped black hair and floppy ears. But she's always done up nice with bows on her ears.

Availability She's already a hot item, and she wouldn't have it any other way.

Value History Unchanged.

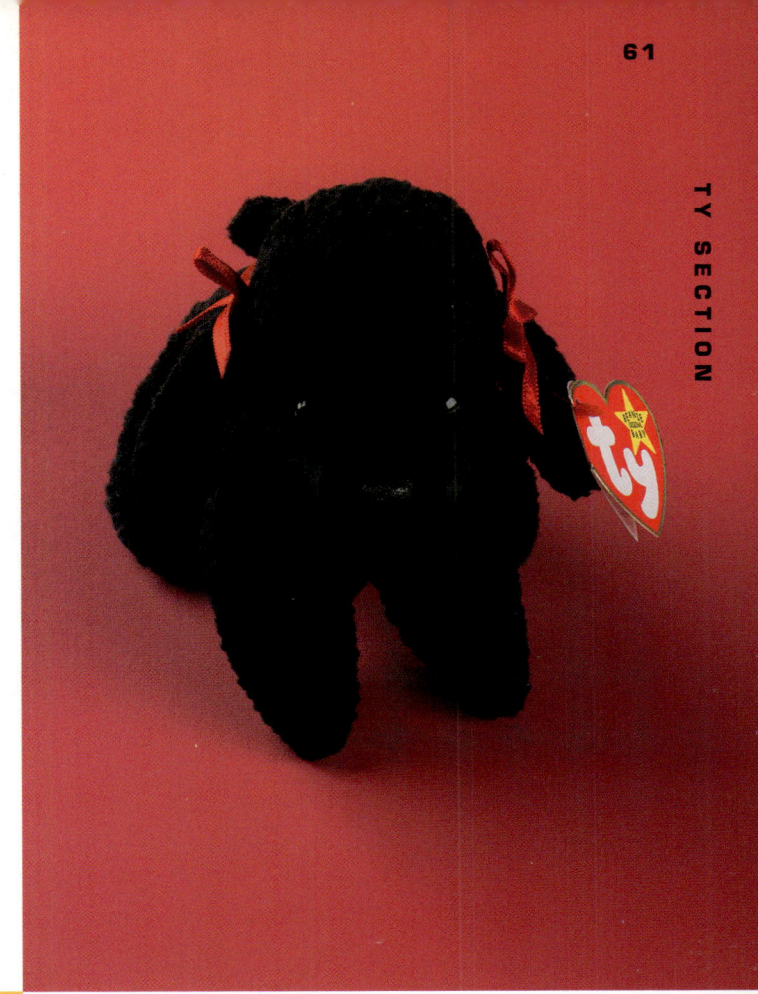

Glory the Bear

Born: July 4, 1997.

Released May 1998.

Description Glory was born on the Fourth of July, and he's certainly a dandy with his blue and red stars and United States flag on his chest. He was no doubt the star attraction at the 1998 Major League All-Star Game, and many collectors already consider him an American treasure.

Availability Only in the United States, and a rare find even there — especially the All-Star Glory.

Value History Unchanged.

TY SECTION

GRACIE THE SWAN

Born June 17, 1996.
Released January 1997.
Retired May 1998.
Description Gracie's entrance onto the Beanie scene was a little clumsy. But she has handled retirement elegantly, leaving her ugly duckling stage and becoming very popular.
Availability Gracie seems to be shy. She makes few appearances.
Value History Increasing.

GOLDIE THE FISH

Born Nov. 14, 1994.
Released 1994.
Retired January 1998.
Description This bright orange swimmer is the last of the Beanie fish to be retired. His Teenie Beanie counterpart was a member of the McDonald's promotion in 1997.
Availability He's a slippery fellow to reel in.
Value History Still inexpensive, but increasing.

Gobbles the Turkey

Born Nov. 27, 1996.

Released October 1997.

Description Gobbles features a lovely tail that fans out in an array of autumn hues. You don't want to have this turkey for Thanksgiving dinner unless you give him a seat at the table.

Availability Gobbled up quickly; catch him when you can.

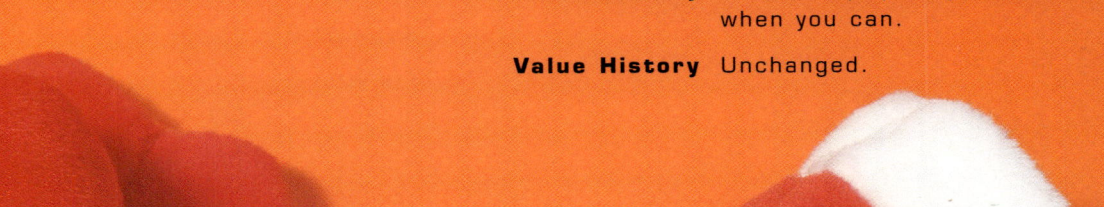

Value History Unchanged.

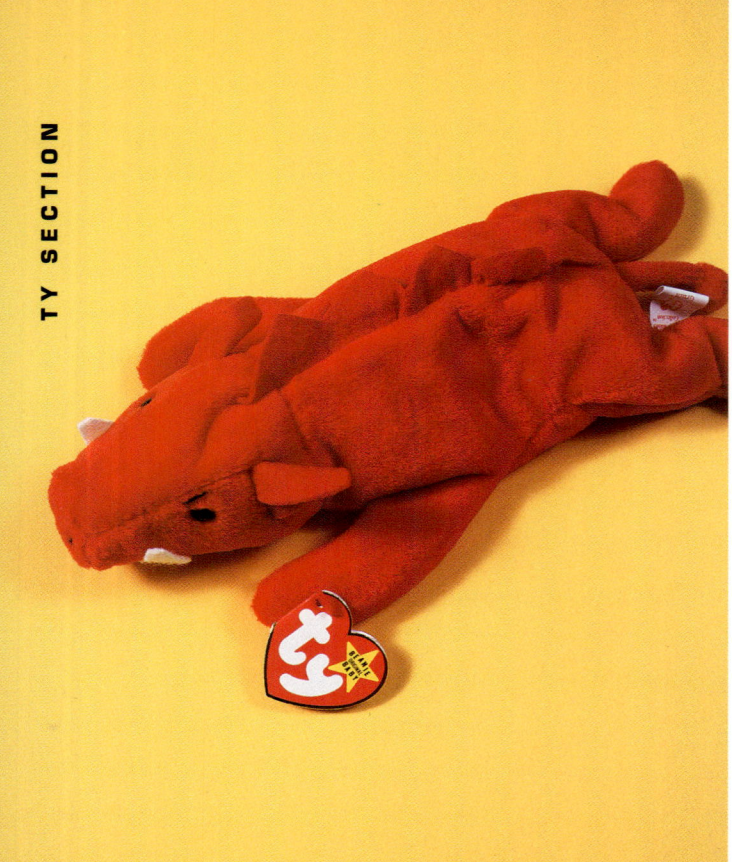

Grunt the Razorback

Born: July 19, 1995.

Released 1995.

Retired May 1997.

Description Although Grunt's debut fell a little flat, those who passed him by are sighing now. Watch for his bright red cloth and two white tusks. And be careful — there have been many counterfeits.

Availability Tough to get hold of.

Value History Somewhat expensive, but stable.

Happy the hippo

Born Feb. 25, 1994.

Released 1994.

Retired May 1998.

Description This leathery gray guy had a production number of about half the normal Beanie production. He was later introduced in lavender, which both boys and girls seem to admire. He has a matching Teenie Beanie and a Pillow Pal named Tubby.

Availability Hippos are hard to hide. Especially lavender ones.

Value History Lavender Happy is much cheaper than gray Happy.

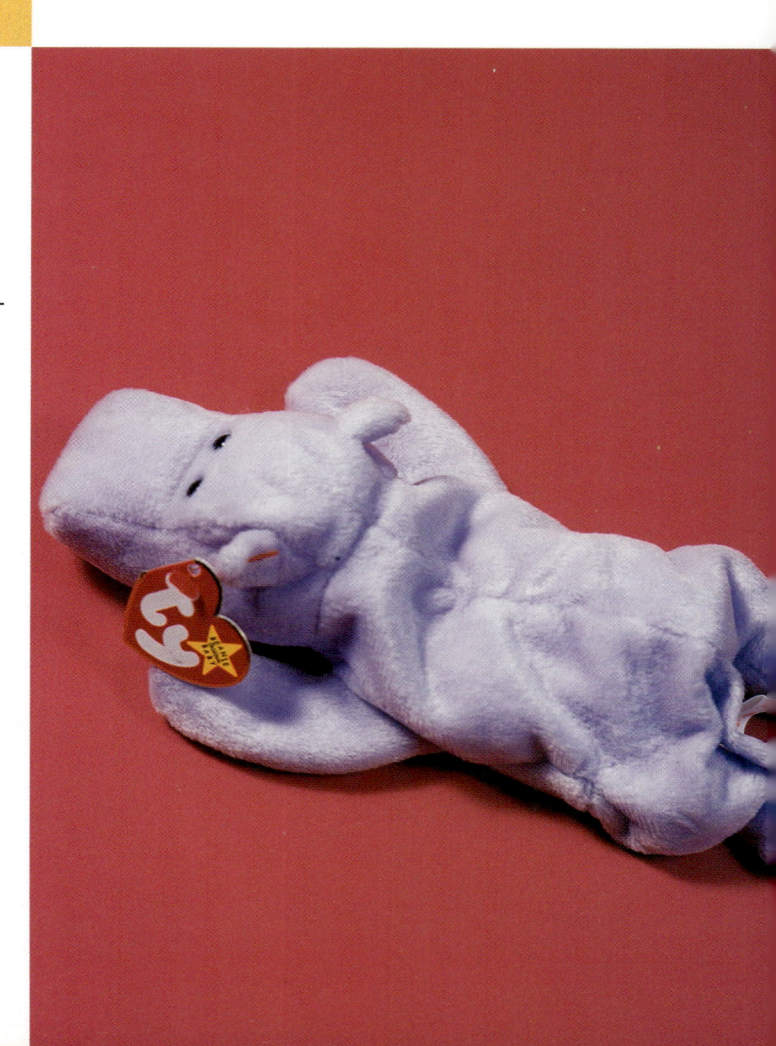

Hippity the Bunny

Born	June 1, 1996.
Released	January 1997.
Retired	May 1998.
Description	When this mint green bunny hit the shelves in 1997, collectors were desperate for him to complete the rabbit line. He is seen less often than the other Beanie rabbits.
Availability	Hard to find, but seems to be showing up more often.
Value History	Inexpensive but increasing.

Hissy the Snake

Born April 4, 1997.

Released January 1998.

Description Hissy's upper portion of plush tie-dyed fabric resembles Bronty. His coils made him the first stretchy Beanie Baby. He is a fun replacement for Slither.

Availability Hissy is moderately easy to find.

Value History Unchanged.

Hoot the Owl

Born Aug. 9, 1995.

Released 1995.

Retired October 1997.

Description Hoot is no wisecracker. He's just an astute fellow in two-tone brown who is more petite than other Beanies.

Availability If you see him, get him before he flies away.

Value History Reasonably priced now, but on the rise.

Hoppity the Bunny

Born April 3, 1996.

Released January 1997.

Retired May 1998.

Description Like other Beanie bunnies, this cotton-candy lookalike was produced for only one year.

Availability Hoppity only shows her face now and then.

Value History Inexpensive but increasing.

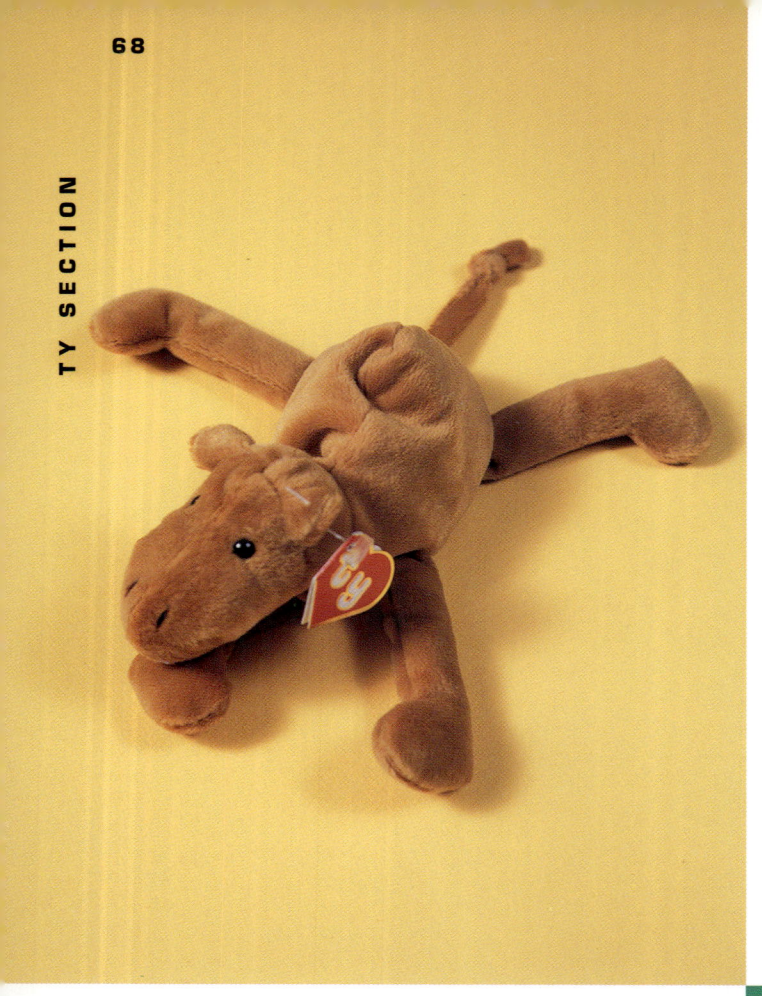

Humphrey the Camel

Born Date unknown.
Released 1994.
Retired 1995.
Description Even with his humpback and wobbly legs, Humphrey is a treasure. He had a low production number and was made for only one year. Many are found worn and damaged from being well-loved.
Availability Humphrey is not plentiful. You'll have to look hard for him.
Value History Very expensive but decreasing.

Inch the Worm

Born Sept. 3, 1995.
Released 1995.
Retired May 1998.
Description Inch really gets around. You can see him dangling from backpacks, car mirrors and baby strollers. He was first released with felt antennae and a third generation tag. The antennae were changed to yarn in 1996.
Availability The first version is scarce, and even the second version is difficult to get.
Value History Increasing. Felt version worth more than yarn version.

Iggy the Iguana

Born Aug. 12, 1997.

Released January 1998.

Description Iggy has fabric similar to Bronty's, and his yellow mouth and eyes are a striking contrast. Some were issued with a Rainbow the Chameleon tag.

Availability Mistagged Iggys are rare, and he is hard to find with the correct tag, too.

Value History Reasonably priced but increasing.

Inky the Octopus

Born Nov. 29, 1994.
Released 1994.
Retired May 1998.
Description Inky has been found with seven or nine legs occasionally. Inkys were first introduced in tan with no poem in their tags, and some had mouths while others didn't. Inky's now hot pink and a fun addition to any collection.
Availability Seven- and nine-legged Inkys are extremely rare, and all tan. Inkys are scarce. Even pink ones are hard to find.
Value History Pink Inkys are moderately priced and rising. Tan or unusual Inkys are expensive.

Jake the Mallard Duck

Born April 16, 1997.
Released May 1998.
Description He's actually a drake, and he's being hunted by more than duck enthusiasts. He sports some beautiful fall colors.
Availability Unusually hard to sight.
Value History Unchanged.

Jabber the Parrot

Born Oct. 10, 1997.

Released May 1998.

Description This parrot's body style resembles Kiwi the Toucan. He is much desired by many collectors.

Availability Even though he's new, he's already hard to get.

Value History Unchanged.

Jolly the Walrus

Born Dec. 2, 1996.

Released May 1997.

Retired May 1998.

Description This pudgy ocean lover is considered a cute short-lived replacement for the more mundane Tusk.

Availability He's out there, but you'll have to work to find him.

Value History Inexpensive but increasing.

Kiwi the Toucan

Born Sept. 16, 1995.
Released 1995.
Retired May 1997.
Description Many inexpensive counterfeits exist of this artfully colored bird. If it seems too good to be true, it probably is.
Availability Hard to find.
Value History Expensive but decreasing.

Kuku the Cockatoo

Born Jan. 5, 1997.
Released May 1998.
Description Ty's new releases are full of our feathered friends, but none are like Kuku. He is the only all-white bird, and he is a delightful portrayal of a Cockatoo with a pink feathered foo-foo on his head.
Availability This bird is a rare breed, at least for now.
Value History Unchanged.

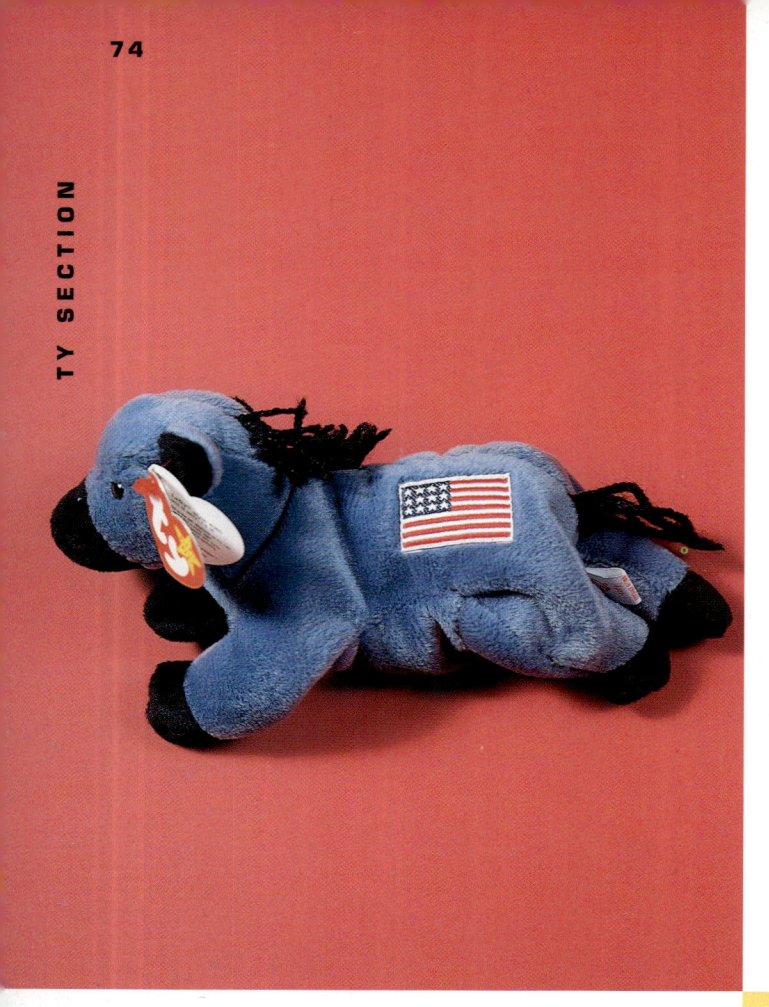

Lefty the Donkey

Born July 4, 1996.

Released Mid-1996.

Retired January 1997.

Description This representative of the Democratic Party was issued for the 1996 presidential election. Some rare Leftys have no flag or an upside-down flag.

Availability Average.

Value History Expensive but decreasing.

Legs the Frog

Born April 25, 1993.

Released 1994.

Retired October 1997.

Description This amphibian was one of the nine original Beanie Babies, and he has been produced with first through fourth generation tags. His flat, green body is popular with boys.

Availability Difficult to find, and first generation Legs is extremely rare.

Value History Moderately priced but increasing.

Libearty the Bear

Born Summer 1996.

Released Mid-1996.

Retired January 1997.

Description Like other Beanies with flags, Libearty has occasionally been found without a flag or with an upside-down flag. She also has been released with a variety of tag errors, including some tags eliminating the Ty Web address on the back.

Availability Libearty can be found in many places.

Value History Expect to pay up to $500 for an erred Libearty.

Lizzy the Lizard

Born May 11, 1995.

Released 1995.

Retired January 1998.

Description Lizzy was first released in tie-dyed cloth but was redesigned in 1996 to look more realistic. Many collectors missed her tie-dyed debut, which puts that version in high demand.

Availability Blue Lizzy is more common than tie-dyed Lizzy.

Value History Tie-dyed and third generation tag Lizzys are very valuable; blue Lizzys are inexpensive.

Lucky the Ladybug

Born May 1, 1995.

Released 1996.

Retired May 1998.

Description Lucky first was released with felt spots that had a tendency to fall off, so she was redesigned with spots that were part of her fabric. Lucky has been produced with varying number of spots. The small-dot Lucky, considered to have 21 dots, is the most rare.

Availability Moderate, but becoming harder to find.

Value History Inexpensive except for the 21-dot version, which can cost up to $800.

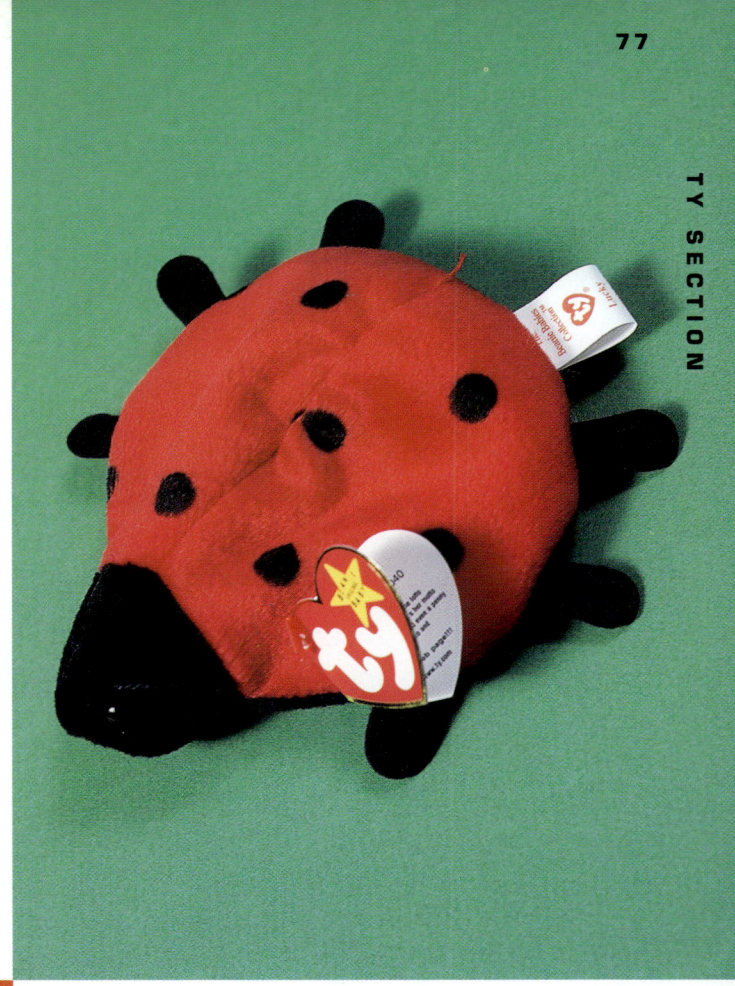

Magic the Dragon

Born Sept. 5, 1995.

Released 1995.

Retired January 1998.

Description He's more fiery than the famous Puff but friendlier than you'd expect. Magic has been released with both light pink and dark pink stitching on his wings.

Availability Trying to find this dragon, you might feel like you're chasing a myth.

Value History Moderately priced but increasing.

TY SECTION

Manny the Manatee

Born June 8, 1995.
Released 1995.
Retired May 1997.
Description At first Manny was considered plain and mundane with his all-gray body and simple face, but now that he's retired he's becoming more and more desirable. Environmentalists love him.
Availability With his popularity, he's becoming harder and harder to find.
Value History Moderately priced and stable.

Maple the Canadian Bear

Born July 1, 1996.
Released January 1997.
Description Maple, first named Pride, represents two important events in Canada: Canadian Independence Day and the Special Olympics. He boasts the Canadian maple leaf flag and a red ribbon.
Availability You might get lucky and find Maple on the U.S. secondary market. Customs has made him very unattainable for Americans in the past.
Value History Price ranges depending on tag, but all Maples are expensive.

Mel the Koala Bear

Born Jan. 15, 1996.

Released January 1997.

Description Mel is just as handsome as the Australian-born actor he is rumored to be named after. He is gray and white with a sweet face and charming smile. He has a matching Teenie Beanie that was part of the McDonald's 1998 promotion.

Availability You don't even have to go down under. This mate is everywhere.

Value History Unchanged.

Mystic the Unicorn

Born May 21, 1994.

Released 1994.

Description This fanciful creature was first produced with a first generation tag, a tail and mane of fine white yarn and a beige horn. He later was issued with a coarse mane and tail, and his horn has now been changed to iridescent.

Availability Mystic is more than a legend. He's real and available if you just believe.

Value History Unchanged.

Nanook the Husky

Born Nov. 21, 1996.

Released May 1997.

Description Even though Nanook is current, shopkeepers can't seem to stock enough of him to satisfy demand. His blue eyes stand out from his dark gray coat with white trim.

Availability This husky doesn't always make himself seen.

Value History Unchanged.

Nip the Cat

Born March 6, 1994.

Released 1994.

Retired January 1998.

Description This golden feline was produced with first through fourth generation tags and underwent several changes before retirement. The first issue of Nip was larger with a white tummy and snout. The second generation Nip, which was produced for only a month, is mostly gold with pink whiskers and nose. He has since been redesigned to seem less floppy, and his paws and the insides of his ears are white.

Availability All versions of Nip are difficult to find, but the second generation version is most rare.

Value History Expect to pay up to $900 for the most rare Nip.

Nuts the Squirrel

Born Jan. 21, 1996.

Released January 1997.

Description This quirky fellow was first produced with big ears and a curvy tail. He later underwent a design change to make his ears smaller and straighten his tail.

Availability Nuts pops up in just about any shop.

Value History Unchanged.

Peace the Bear

Born Feb. 1, 1996.

Released May 1997.

Description Peace is the result of a redesign of Garcia the bear thought to be influenced by Jerry Garcia's family. He holds his own with his stitched peace sign, and many collectors can't get enough of him.

Availability Shopkeepers originally were allowed to order just 36 at a time, putting him in high demand. He's gotten a little more available since then.

Value History Moderately priced and stable.

Patti the Platypus

Born Jan. 6, 1993.

Released 1994.

Retired May 1998.

Description Patti debuted in magenta as one of the first nine Beanie Babies. She has since been released in three other colors: raspberry, dark purple and purple.

Availability Patti can be hard to find.

Value History The purple Patti is reasonably priced, but expect to pay up to $1,100 for a raspberry version. Both are holding steady.

TY SECTION

PEKING THE PANDA BEAR

Born Date unknown.
Released 1994.
Retired 1996.
Description Much like Chilly and Bronty, many people didn't know what they had in Peking. It's now difficult to find Peking without his black-and-white fur being damaged. For that reason, collectors are usually willing to purchase a near mint condition Peking without a tag.
Availability A mint condition Peking is extremely hard to find.
Value History This bear is expensive, but prices seem to be decreasing.

PINCHERS THE LOBSTER

Born June 19, 1993.
Released 1994.
Retired May 1998.
Description This fiery red lobster was first issued with the name Pincher, but an "s" was quickly added to his name. He was one of the first nine Beanie Babies, and he was issued and retired without a poem.
Availability Pinchers is available, but you might have to do some looking.
Value History He's priced well, and he's holding stable.

Peanut the Elephant

Born Jan. 25, 1995.

Released 1995.

Retired May 1998.

Description Peanut first appeared in royal blue, but his color was changed to light blue after only one month. He has a matching Teenie Beanie and a Pillow Pal named Squirt.

Availability Peanut in any color is difficult to get.

Value History Light blue Peanut is inexpensive, but expect to pay up to $5,200 for royal blue Peanut. And that price is rising.

Pinky the Flamingo

Born Feb. 13, 1995.

Released 1995.

Description Pinky's pretty hue makes her popular with girls. She has a matching Teenie Beanie that's even more beloved.

Availability Easy to find and stands out in a crowd.

Value History Unchanged.

Pouch the Kangaroo

Born Nov. 6, 1996.

Released January 1997.

Description Pouch, a devoted mother, was originally issued with her baby attached by a plastic tie. After it was determined that the removable baby was not safe for human kids, Ty began sewing the little kangaroo into Mommy's pouch.

Availability Fluctuates from plentiful to rare.

Value History Unchanged.

Pounce the Cat

Born Aug. 28, 1997.

Released January 1998.

Description This tie-dyed brown feline is a happy member of the Ty cat clan.

Availability Pounce can be found in many places.

Value History Unchanged.

Prance the Cat

Born Nov. 20, 1997.
Released January 1998.
Description Prance cuts a striking pose in his gray coat and dark gray stripes.
Availability He shouldn't be too hard to get hold of.
Value History Unchanged.

Pugsly the Pug Dog

Born May 2, 1996.
Released May 1997.
Description He was issued on Mother's Day, and this pug's mug is one any mother could love.
Availability Sometimes hard to find.
Value History Unchanged.

Princess the Bear

Born Date unknown.

Released October 1997.

Description Princess was issued as a memorial after the tragic death of another princess: Princess Diana of Wales. All proceeds from the sale of the bear were donated to the Diana, Princess of Wales Memorial Fund. Some speculators say that the poem printed in special font will no longer appear on the swing tag, which could lead to a price increase.

Availability This special tribute Beanie is highly sought after and hard to find.

Value History Princess is moderately priced and decreasing, for now.

Puffer the Puffin

Born Nov. 3, 1997.
Released January 1998.
Description What is a Puffin? Well, it's a bird. And a more colorful one you won't often see. Puffer's body resembles Caw, but his coloring is all his own.
Availability He's easier to find some times than others.
Value History Unchanged.

Radar the Bat

Born Oct. 30, 1995.
Released 1995.
Retired May 1997.
Description This realistic bat was released for Halloween. Radar's first retirement lasted one day because of collectors' mad dash to acquire the suddenly retired bat. He was issued with third and fourth generation tags.

Quackers the Duck

Born April 19, 1994.

Released 1994.

Retired May 1998.

Description When he debuted, this duck was going — that is, flying — nowhere. Quackers was first issued with no wings, and he had a different name: Quacker. He has since added an "s" to his name and some wings to make him look a little less awkward. He can be found with Quacker printed on first and second generation tags.

Availability The wingless version is rare, but the second version is moderately available.

Value History Wingless is expensive and increasing; winged is inexpensive and stable.

Rainbow the Chameleon

Born Oct. 14, 1997.

Released January 1998.

Description Imagine mistaking a chameleon for an iguana! It happened to Rainbow. Many copies of this chameleon had Iggy the Iguana's name on the swing tag and tush tag. So many were produced that the mismarked lizard isn't rare enough to follow the price escalation trend.

Availability Rainbow sometimes blends in; you'll have to look hard for him.

Value History Unchanged.

Rex the Tyrannosaurus

Born Date unknown.

Released 1995.

Retired January 1996.

Description Although he is the most plentiful of his dinosaur brothers, he is still a red-hot item. He was released without a birthday alongside Steg and Bronty in 1995.

Availability Like all dinosaurs, you don't see one every day.

Value History Expensive, but decreasing.

Righty the Elephant

Born July 4, 1996.

Released 1996.

Retired January 1997.

Description He shares a birthday with the United States, and he bears its flag. Righty was released to represent the Republican Party during the 1996 presidential elections. He and his cousin, Lefty, cross party lines in that they share their birthday and their poem.

Availability He can usually be found.

Value History Somewhat expensive but decreasing.

Ringo the Raccoon

Born July 14, 1995.

Released 1995.

Description Although Ringo is still very popular, he probably has seen his hey day. Children find his striped tail a lot of fun.

Availability Ringo is easy to find now, but his popularity might make him rare after he's retired.

Value History Unchanged.

Rocket the Blue Jay

Born March 12, 1997.

Released May 1998.

Description Rocket is one of many Beanie birds released in 1998. He supposedly gets his name from the blue jay's tremendous capability for speed — not for a certain Toronto pitcher. His design is similar to Caw, and he is highly sought after by bird lovers.

Availability Even though he's a new release, Rocket is unusually hard to find.

Value History Unchanged.

Roary the Lion

Born Feb. 20, 1996.

Released 1997.

Description Roary was the first Beanie to have "fur," and that's not even his calling card. This Beanie was lucky enough to make an appearance on NBC's Today Show with Ty Vice President Carmen Kohlwes. Roary was also given away at a 1997 Kansas City Royals baseball game.

Availability Roary usually makes himself known.

Value History Steady, reasonable price.

ROVER THE DOG

Born May 30, 1996.

Released Mid-1996.

Retired May 1998.

Description Rover is loved by collectors of all ages. He reminds children of another big red dog, Clifford. And he reminds older adults of a children's game, "Red Rover, Red Rover . . ."

Availability Rover is about as hard to find as a red dog should be.

Value History Very inexpensive now, but increasing.

Scottie the Terrier

Born June 15, 1996.

Released Mid-1996.

Retired May 1998.

Description Although Scottie officially was born on June 15, 1996, there are a few Scotties with tags that say his birth date is June 3, 1996. Either way, the all-black Scottie was one of the first Beanies with napped hair.

Availability This terrier is not easy to nab.

Value History Inexpensive now, but Scottie's price is on the rise.

Scoop the Pelican

Born July 1, 1996.

Released Mid-1996.

Description With his long, orange bill and his large wings, Scoop is a favorite among Floridians. He also has a matching Teenie Beanie that was part of the McDonald's Happy Meal promotion.

Availability Scoop is everywhere.

Value History Unchanged.

Seamore the White Seal

Born Dec. 14, 1996.

Released 1994.

Retired October 1997.

Description Seamore's glistening white coat makes him difficult to keep clean. Nevertheless, McDonald's included him as a Teenie Beanie is the fast-food restaurant's 1997 promotion. He also has a matching Ty plush named Misty.

Availability Seamores in mint condition are rare. Otherwise, he's moderately easy to find.

Value History Expect to pay up to $225.

Seaweed the Otter

Born March 19, 1996.

Released January 1996.

Description Seaweed, who is made of felt, is one Beanie that needs protection. Even though otters usually love water, be sure not to get this one wet.

Availability Seaweed gets snapped up in a hurry.

Value History Unchanged.

Slither the Snake

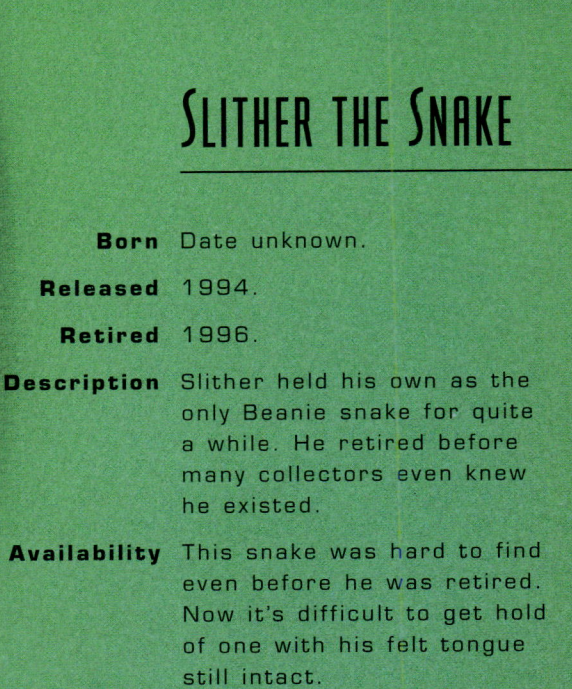

Born	Date unknown.
Released	1994.
Retired	1996.
Description	Slither held his own as the only Beanie snake for quite a while. He retired before many collectors even knew he existed.
Availability	This snake was hard to find even before he was retired. Now it's difficult to get hold of one with his felt tongue still intact.
Value History	Expect to pay up to $2,500 for this rare reptile.

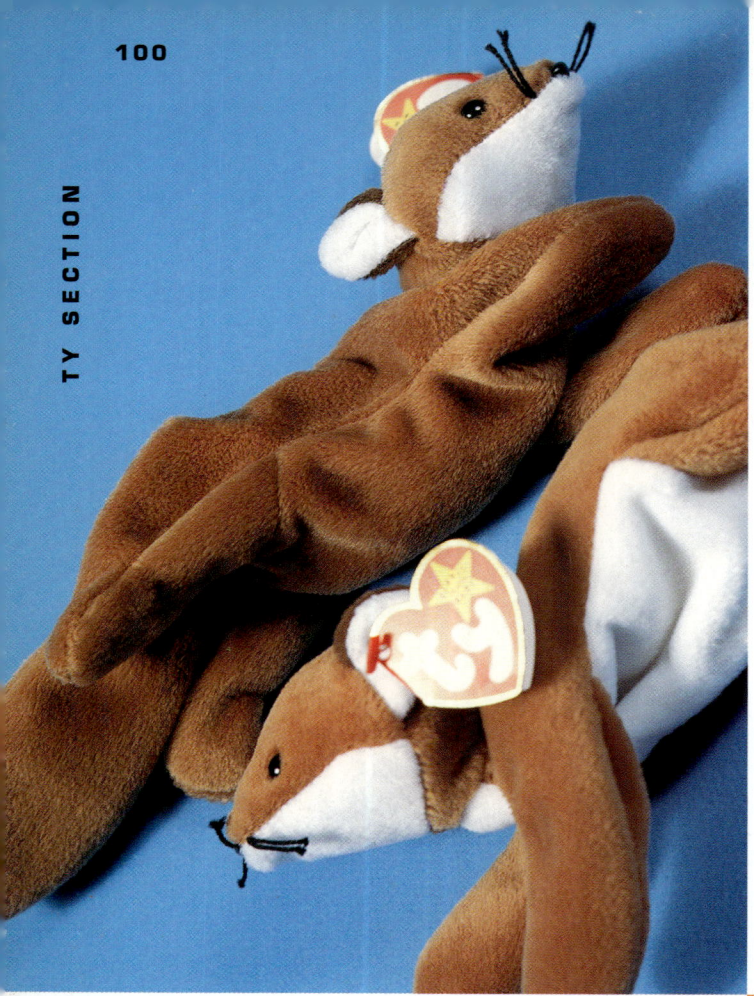

Sly the Fox

Born Sept. 12, 1996.

Released Mid-1996.

Description When Sly was first introduced, he had a brown belly. But less than a month later, he was redesigned with a white tummy. Sly has a matching Pillow Pal named Foxy.

Availability Brown-bellied Sly is rare, but the white-bellied version is common.

Value History Expect to pay up to $250 for the more limited version. The white-bellied Sly is unchanged.

Snip the Siamese Cat

Born Oct. 22, 1996.

Released January 1997.

Description Snip is a well-bred feline, and he is the only Siamese of the Beanie clan. His characteristic brown highlights give him distinction — and personality. He has a matching Pillow Pal named Meow.

Availability Look for this Siamese, if you please, and you will probably find him.

Value History Unchanged.

Smoochy the Frog

Born Oct. 1, 1997.

Released January 1998.

Description Smoochy's body has more shape and color than his retired brother, Legs. His original string mouth was short-lived, however. He soon was redesigned with a felt mouth.

Availability Smoochy is easy to net.

Value History Unchanged.

Snort the Bull

Born May 15, 1995.

Released January 1997.

Description Snort is a redesign of Tabasco the Bull, who was renamed to avoid infringing on the Tabasco hot sauce trademark. Unlike Tabasco, Snort has beige hooves. With his red body, he still makes a great mascot for the Chicago Bulls professional basketball team.

Availability Snort is moderately available.

Value History Unchanged.

Snowball the Snowman

Born Dec. 22, 1996.

Released October 1997.

Retired January 1998.

Description Snowball, one of just two Beanies that aren't animals, showed up on the secondary market at a high price.

Availability Just when you think you might see this snowman, he melts away.

Value History Moderately priced but increasing.

Sparky
the Dalmatian

Born Feb. 27, 1996.

Released 1996.

Retired May 1997.

Description You're not seeing double. Sparky looks remarkably like Dotty the Dalmatian. Sparky has the same name as the mascot for the National Fire Protection Association, and the word is that his name was the reason for his quick retirement.

Availability Sparky is out there, just don't confuse him with Dotty.

Value History You can get this dog for less than $200, and his price is holding steady.

Spinner the Spider

Born Oct. 28, 1996.

Released October 1997.

Description Spinner and Batty the bat were released about the same time — just in time for Halloween. The two make a delightfully frightening team.

Availability If you don't see Spinner on the shelf, look up. She might be spinning a web overhead. Either place, she should be easy to catch.

Value History Unchanged.

Speedy the Turtle

Born Aug. 14, 1994.

Released 1994.

Retired October 1997.

Description Speedy has a matching Teenie Beanie, but his Beanie Baby version is not much bigger. He's one of the smaller in the Ty Beanie line, and he's quick to warm your heart.

Availability Catch this turtle if you can.

Value History Inexpensive now, but get him fast. His value is increasing.

Spike the Rhinoceros

Born Aug. 13, 1996.

Released Mid-1996.

Description This guy might look tough, but he's harmless as a mouse. As a matter of fact, he features the same gray fabric as his rodent friend, Trap.

Availability This rhino should be easy to see; his horn usually stands out in a crowd.

Value History Unchanged.

Splash
the Orca Whale

Born July 8, 1993.

Released 1994.

Retired May 1997.

Description This whale did make a splash as one of the original nine Beanie Babies. She paved the way for her sister, Waves. Although she's popular, you won't find any airplanes dedicated to her — yet.

Availability Splash surfaces now and then.

Value History Somewhat expensive.

Spooky the Ghost

Born Oct. 31, 1995.

Released 1995.

Retired January 1998.

Description Spooky, who brightened up the Halloween gloom in 1995, and his Christmas cousin Snowball the Snowman are the only Beanies that aren't animals. Spooky was first produced with his name missing the "y" on the swing tag and with a felt mouth that easily fell off. He's been produced with three different mouth styles.

Availability Spooky, like most ghosts, rarely makes himself visible.

Value History Somewhat inexpensive now, but increasing.

Spot the Dog

Born Jan. 3, 1993.

Released 1994.

Retired October 1997.

Description Spot, one of the original nine Beanies, is the oldest of the Beanie family: over 35 in dog years. This white pup was first produced without a spot on his back.

Availability If you spot one without a spot, grab him. He comes a little easier with a spot.

Value History Expect to pay up to $2,500 for a spotless Spot. The latter version is moderately priced.

Spunky the Cocker Spaniel

Born Jan. 14, 1997.

Released January 1998.

Description This rowdy pup is designed similarly to his canine cousin, Bones. Just like a real Cocker Spaniel, Spunky sports wavy fur on his ears.

Availability If you call for this doggie long enough, he's sure to come.

Value History Unchanged.

Squealer the Pig

Born April 23, 1993.

Released 1994.

Retired May 1998.

Description Squealer was one of the original nine Beanies, and his knotted tail makes him a fun addition to any collection. He also has a matching Pillow Pal named Oink.

Availability Finding this pig in a pile might be like looking for a needle in a haystack.

Value History Moderately inexpensive now, but expect that to increase.

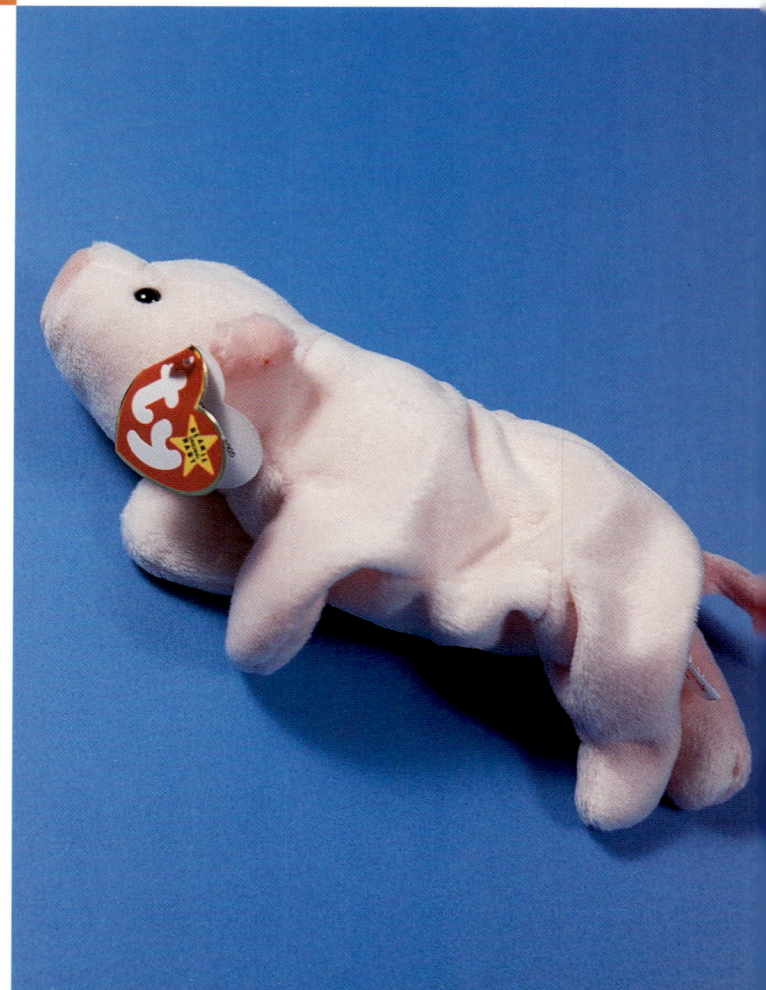

Steg
the Stegosaurus

Born Date unknown.
Released 1995.
Retired January 1996.
Description This muted gold, blue and green dinosaur retired quickly and never had a poem. He is one of the most popular of the Beanie dinos, along with Rex.
Availability Not as plentiful as he once was. Let's hope he doesn't become extinct.
Value History Up to $1,200 but look for the price to drop.

TY SECTION

Sting the Ray

Born Aug. 27, 1995.

Released 1995.

Retired January 1997.

Description This ocean dweller is a loner type, and with a lot of handling his delicate seams might come apart. For that reason, Sting in mint condition is rare. His tie-dyed fabric resembles that of Bronte, and Sting is popular with boys.

Availability You may have to keep your line in the water for a while before you reel in this one. Sting with a third-generation tag is especially scarce.

Value History Priced up to $250 and holding.

Stinger the Scorpion

Born Sept. 29, 1997.

Released May 1998.

Description Stinger sports a silvery brown material that is new to Beanie land. His fabric stinger, two large claws and a stinger tail make him as creepy as the real thing.

Availability Stinger is hard to find, but if you see him be careful not to get stung.

Value History Unchanged.

STINKY THE SKUNK

Born Feb. 13, 1995.

Released 1995.

Description Following in the footsteps of another famous suave skunk, Stinky is the Don Juan of Beanies. Who could resist falling in love with him?

Availability His striped head pops up everywhere.

Value History Current.

Stripes the tiger

Born June 11, 1995.

Released 1995.

Retired May 1998.

Description Stripes was active only three years before retirement, but he stayed very busy with three design changes. The first Stripes was gold and black and lacked a poem. The second version had a fuzzy striped fabric on his belly, making him highly sought after. The final version lightened the colors to caramel and black, making the stripes seem thinner.

Availability All versions of this tiger are hard to hunt down, but the fuzzy-bellied version is extremely rare.

Value History The most recent version is inexpensive, but the other styles of Stripes are costly.

Stretch the Ostrich

Born Sept. 21, 1997.

Released January 1998.

Description Stretch is a favorite among many collectors. She is artistically designed and quite the lady with her long legs and glamorous white fur collar.

Availability Stretch often buries her head in the sand.

Value History Unchanged.

Strut the Rooster

Born March 8, 1996.

Released 1997.

Description Strut shares the same birthday and poem with his predecessor, Doodles, but Strut's coloring is a little brighter. Otherwise, the two birds are identical.

Availability Strut is available in many shops, but not all.

Value History Unchanged.

Tank the Armadillo

Born Feb. 22, 1995.

Released 1995.

Retired October 1997.

Description Through three redesigns, Tank became more and more realistic. The first version had a shell with seven plates, and the second version's shell had nine plates. The Tank tale is that a Texas collector wrote to Ty offering advice on what a real armadillo looks like, resulting in the final redesign. The final version of Tank features a smaller body with ears that sit higher on his head. Also, more attention was given to detail.

Availability Armadillos are always on the go. It might take some time to chase this one down.

Value History The latest and most inexpensive version can cost up to $80, and that price is increasing.

Tabasco the Bull

Born May 15, 1995.

Released 1995.

Retired January 1997.

Description The color of Tabasco's hooves differs from Snort. Tabasco reportedly was retired early to avoid a confrontation with the Tabasco hot sauce company.

Availability Tabasco is a hot item and hard to get a taste of.

Value History Price fluctuates, but expect to pay more than $100 for him.

Tracker the Basset Hound

Born June 5, 1997.

Released May 1998.

Description This hound's cute face could easily be the doggie in the window. He has a matching Ty plush named Sherlock.

Availability Hard to find, but he's already made his way to the secondary market.

Value History Unchanged.

Old Face Teddy Bears

Born Date unknown.

Released Mid-1994.

Retired 1995.

Description For each of the six colors, 50,000 of these bears were produced with European/Victorian style faces. The old-faced bears feature longer snouts with eyes spread far apart. It's hard to believe these bears once sold for $5 or $6 each.

Availability Old Face teddy bears may require some searching, but they're out there. The brown Teddy is the rarest.

Value History They once sold for $5, but now they're priced in the thousands. Expect to pay up to $4,000 for the brown Old Face teddy.

Teddy the Brown Bear

Born Dec. 28, 1995.

Released 1996.

Retired January 1998.

Description This new-faced brown napped bear wears a cranberry colored ribbon around his neck. He was retired later than the other colors of new-faced Beanie Baby bears.

Availability Teddy's availability fluctuates.

Value History Expect to pay about $100, a price that should increase.

New Face Teddy Bears

Born Date unknown.

Released 1995.

Retired 1996.

Description Ty became its own competitor in 1995 when it produced new-faced bears in the same colors of its old-faced bears.

Availability New Face teddy bears are very hard to find.

Value History Same as old-faced counterparts with the exception of the cheaper brown teddy.

Trap the Mouse

Born Date unknown.
Released 1994.
Retired 1995.
Description His simple design might have moved many collectors to pass him by. They're kicking themselves now.
Availability Almost impossible to trap this mouse.
Value History He's a simple mouse, but expect to pay up to $2,200.

Tusk the Walrus

Born Sept. 18, 1995.
Released 1995.
Retired January 1997.
Description Tusk had a hard time with his name when he was first released. Some pieces were issued with the name "Tuck." Others were produced with the tusks pointing upward. Tusk shares his body style with Seamore the Seal.
Availability Tusk is moderately available, but the Tuck version is rare.
Value History Somewhat expensive but decreasing.

Tuffy
the Brown Terrier

Born Oct. 12, 1996.

Released May 1997.

Description This beige-and-brown pup is one of the five Beanies with napped fur. The others are Curly the bear, Scottie the terrier, Fleece the lamb and Gigi the poodle, which is newly released.

Availability You can find Tuffy if you work at it.

Twigs the Giraffe

Born May 19, 1995.
Released 1995.
Retired May 1998.
Description Twigs has been seen in varying shades of orange. He also has a matching Teenie Beanie that was part of the McDonald's Happy Meal promotion.
Availability Twigs may soon be a tall order to fill thanks to his retirement.
Value History Inexpensive now but increasing.

Valentino the Bear

Born Feb. 14, 1994.

Released 1994.

Description This lover wears his true feelings on his chest. Valentino, who was named for the legendary Rudolph Valentino of the silent screen era, was born on Valentine's Day. He has been involved in many Help the Children projects.

Availability Valentino's availability fluctuates, but he is especially hard to find with a second generation swing tag.

Value History Inexpensive.

Velvet the Panther

Born Dec. 16, 1995.

Released 1995.

Retired October 1997.

Description Velvet's shiny black coat emphasizes his shocking eyes. Many Velvets have off-center noses.

Availability Many shops will have Velvet in stock.

Value History He's beautiful AND cheap.

Waddle the Penguin

Born Dec. 19, 1995.

Released 1995.

Retired May 1998.

Description Waddle gets a lot of his attitude from the yellow bib around his neck. He's a hard penguin to ignore. He also has a matching Teenie Beanie and a Ty plush named Shivers.

Availability This penguin is hard to pin down.

Value History Inexpensive now but increasing.

WAVES THE ORCA WHALE

Born Dec. 8, 1996.

Released May 1997.

Retired May 1998.

Description Some of these whales were found with the name Echo on the swing tag. Echo is actually a curvy dolphin that was introduced when Waves retired.

Availability Waves with either name on the tag is a difficult acquisition.

Value History Both versions are inexpensive now, but expect the mismatched pair of Waves and Echo to increase in value.

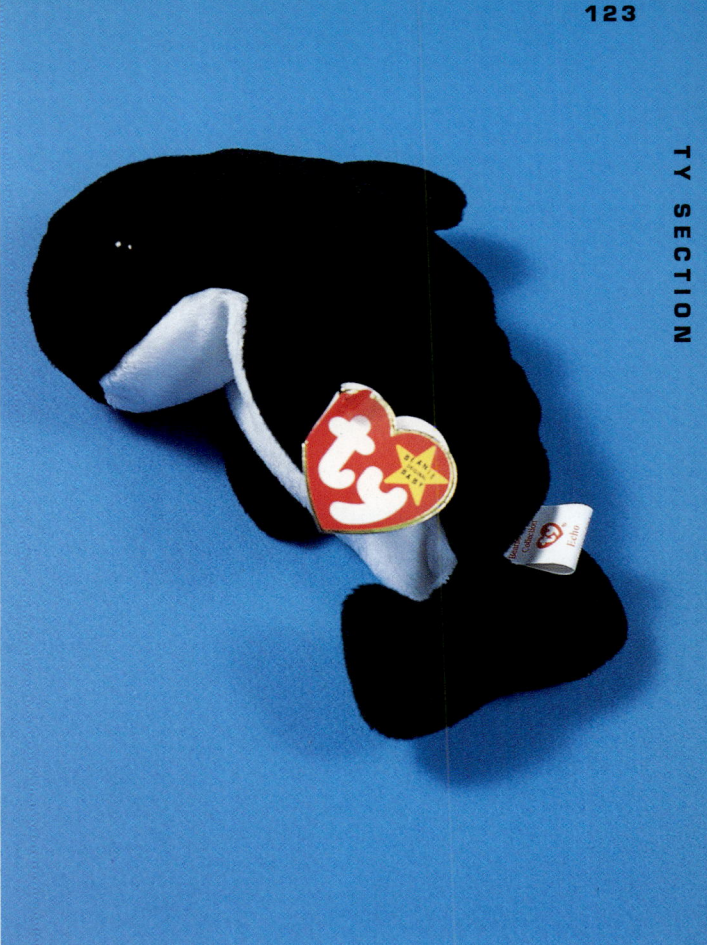

WEB THE SPIDER

Born Date unknown.

Released 1994.

Retired 1995.

Description Web was Ty's first attempt at a Beanie spider, and he was issued without a poem. When Spinner replaced Web in 1997, many collectors were delighted because they had not had the chance to buy Web.

Availability This spider is a hard one to trap.

Value History Up to $1,800 and holding.

Weenie the Dog

Born July 20, 1995.
Released 1996.
Retired May 1998.
Description This down-to-earth dachshund looks like he could brighten anyone's day. Put him in a race against other Beanie breeds, and he's sure to outperform his name.
Availability This is one slippery dog.
Value History He's inexpensive now, but he's turning heads. Expect his worth to rise.

Whisper the Deer

Born April 5, 1997.
Released May 1998.
Description This deer is a dear with her white spots, tummy and chest. Her body style resembles Twigs, who was retired at the same time Whisper was released.
Availability Very hard to find immediately after release.
Value History Unchanged.

Wise the Owl

Born May 31, 1997.

Released May 1998.

Description Looking great in '98. That should be the motto for Wise, whose graduation cap commemorates his release year.

Availability Difficult to get now, but he'll be even more rare after the new year.

Value History Already above new release value, but still reasonable.

WRINKLES THE BULLDOG

Born May 1, 1996.

Released Mid-1996.

Description The intricate design of this pup shows off some of Ty's best craftsmanship. He has a matching Pillow Pal named Bruiser and a Ty plush friend named Winston.

Availability Varies.

Value History Unchanged.

Ziggy the Zebra

Born Dec. 24, 1995.

Released 1995.

Retired May 1998.

Description This African native was originally smaller and had more white space between his black stripes. He has a matching Pillow Pal named Zulu.

Availability Ever try to catch a zebra? It's not impossible.

Value History Inexpensive and stable.

Zip the Cat

Born March 28, 1994.

Released 1995.

Retired May 1998.

Description The first Zip was larger and featured a black-and-white belly and a triangle on his snout. The second was all black with pink ears and nose. The final had white ears, paws and whiskers.

Availability This kitty requires a lot of searching.

Value History For the rarer second version, expect to pay up to $2,000. And the price is increasing.

Ty Price Guide

What the Columns Mean

The LO and HI columns reflect current retail selling ranges. The HI column generally represents full retail selling prices. The LO column generally represents the lowest price one could expect to find with extensive shopping.

1993-98 Beanie Babies

Ally the alligator . . . . 35.00 . . . . 60.00
Born 3/14/94
Retired

Ants the anteater . . . . 8.00 . . . . 20.00
Born 11/7/97

Baldy the eagle . . . . 10.00 . . . . 20.00
Born 2/17/96
Retired

Baldy the eagle . . . . 175.00 . . . 250.00
w/76ers card, Retired

Batty the bat . . . . 6.00 . . . . 15.00
Born 10/29/96
Retired

Batty the Bat . . . . 50.00 . . .100.00
w/Brewers card

Bernie the St. Bernard . . . . . . 6.00 . . . . 12.00
Born 10/3/96

Bessie the cow . . . . 50.00 . . . . 80.00
Born 6/27/95
Retired

Blackie the bear . . . . 6.00 . . . . 15.00
Born 7/15/94

Blizzard the white tiger . . . . . 10.00 . . . . 25.00
Born 12/12/96
Retired

Blizzard the white tiger . . . . . 75.00 . . . 125.00
w/White Sox card

Bones the dog . . . . .10.00 . . . . 20.00
Born 1/18/94
Retired

Bongo the monkey . . . . 45.00 . . . . 80.00
w/Brown tail

Bongo the monkey . . . . 75.00 . . . 125.00
w/Tan tail 3rd gen tag
b/w tush tag, Retired

Bongo the monkey . . . . 60.00 . . . . 90.00
w/Tan tail 3rd gen tag
red/white tush tag, Retired

Bongo the monkey . . . . 6.00 . . . . 12.00
w/Tan tail 4th gen tag
Born 8/17/95

Bongo the monkey . . . . . . 3200.00 . . 4000.00
w/Nana tag, Retired

Bongo the monkey . . . . 75.00 . . . 150.00
w/Brewers card

Brittania the bear . . . . 450.00 . . . 600.00
Born 12/15/97

Bronty the brontosaurus . . 800.00 . . 1350.00
Retired

Bruno the terrier . . . . 6.00 . . . . 12.00
Born 9/9/97

Bubbles the fish . . . . 125.00 . . . 200.00
Born 7/2/95
Retired

Bucky the beaver . . . . 25.00 . . . . 40.00
Born 6/8/95
Retired

Bumble the bee . . . . 500.00 . . . 800.00
Retired

Caw the crow . . . . 600.00 . . . 900.00
Retired

Chilly the polar bear . . . . . 1800.00 . . 2500.00
Retired

Chip the cat . . . . 7.50 . . . . 15.00
Born 1/26/96

Chocolate the moose .... 6.00 .... 15.00
Born 4/27/93

Chocolate the moose ..... 100.00 ... 175.00
w/Nuggets card #'d/5000

Chops the lamb .... 150.00 ... 225.00
Born 5/3/96
Retired

Claude the crab .... 7.50 .... 15.00
Born 9/3/96

Claude the crab .... 15.00 .... 40.00
w/all caps

Congo the gorilla .... 6.00 .... 12.00
Born 11/9/96

Congo the gorilla .... 200.00 ... 300.00
w/Toy Fair ribbon

Coral the fish .... 150.00 ... 225.00
Born 3/2/95
Retired

Crunch the shark .... 6.00 .... 15.00
Born 1/13/96

Cubbie the bear .... 15.00 .... 30.00
Born 11/14/93
Retired

Cubbie the bear .... 4000.00 .. 5000.00
w/Brownie tag, Retired

Cubbie the bear .... 150.00 ... 225.00
w/May Cubs card, Retired

Cubbie the bear .... 125.00 ... 200.00
w/Sept. Cubs card, Retired

Curly the bear .... 10.00 .... 25.00
Born 4/12/96

Curly the bear .... 150.00 ... 300.00
w/Spurs card #'d/2500

Daisy the cow .... 6.00 .... 15.00
Born 5/10/94

Daisy the cow .... 350.00 ... 550.00
w/Harry Caray tag
Cubs card #'d/10000

Derby the horse .... 8.00 .... 20.00
w/coarse mane and white patch

Derby the horse .... 15.00 .... 30.00
w/coarse mane and w/o star

Derby the horse .... 3500.00 .. 5000.00
w/fine mane

Digger the red crab ...... 90.00 ... 150.00
Born 8/23/95
Retired

Digger the orange crab ... 500.00 ... 800.00
Retired

Doby the doberman .... 6.00 .... 12.00
Born 10/9/96

Doodle the rooster .... 30.00 .... 50.00
Born 3/8/96
Retired

Dotty the dalmation ...... 6.00 .... 12.00
Born 10/17/96

Early the robin .... 12.00 .... 20.00
Born 2/20/97

Ears the bunny .... 8.00 .... 20.00
Born 4/18/95
Retired

Echo the dolphin .... 10.00 .... 20.00
Born 12/21/96
Retired

Echo the dolphin
w/Waves tag, Retired ..... 10.00 .... 25.00

Erin the bear .... 40.00 .... 80.00
Born 3/17/97

Flash the dolphin .... 90.00 ... 150.00
Born 5/13/93
Retired

Fetch the golden retreiver ... 10.00 .... 20.00
Born 2/4/97

Fleece the lamb .... 6.00 .... 12.00
Born 3/21/96

Flip the cat .... 25.00 .... 40.00
Born 2/28/95
Retired

Floppity the bunny .... 8.00 .... 20.00
Born 5/28/96
Retired

Flutter the butterfly .... 800.00 .. 1400.00
Retired

Fortune the panda .... 40.00 .... 60.00
Born 12/6/97

Freckles the leopard ...... 6.00 .... 12.00
Born 6/3/96

Garcia the bear .... 150.00 ... 225.00
Born 8/1/95
Retired

Gigi the poodle .... 10.00 .... 25.00
Born 3/7/97

Glory the bear .... 100.00 ... 150.00
Born 7/4/97

Glory the bear .... 300.00 ... 400.00
w/All-Star card

Gobbles the turkey .... 8.00 .... 20.00
Born 11/27/96

Goldie the goldfish .... 30.00 .... 50.00
Born 11/14/94
Retired

Gracie the swan .... 8.00 .... 20.00
Born 6/17/96
Retired

Grunt the razorback ...... 150.00 ... 225.00
Born 7/19/95
Retired

Happy the lavender hippo .... 12.00 .... 20.00
Born 2/25/94
Retired

Happy the gray hippo ...... 550.00 ... 850.00
Retired

Hippity the bunny .... 8.00 .... 20.00
Born 6/1/96
Retired

Hissy the snake .... 6.00 .... 15.00
Born 4/4/97

Hissy the snake .... 75.00 ... 150.00
w/Diamondbacks card

Hoot the owl .... 30.00 .... 50.00
Born 8/9/95
Retired

Hoppity the bunny .... 8.00 .... 20.00
Born 4/3/96
Retired

Humphrey the camel ..... 1800.00 .. 2500.00
Retired

Iggy the iguana .... 8.00 .... 20.00
Born 8/12/97

Iggy the iguana .... 6.00 .... 12.00
w/tongue

Inch the worm w/felt ant. ... 150.00 ... 250.00
Retired

Inch the worm w/yarn ant. ... 10.00 .... 20.00
Born 9/3/95
Retired

Inky the pink octopus ...... 20.00 .... 35.00
Retired

Inky the tan octopus ...... 550.00 ... 800.00

w/mouth
Retired

Inky the tan octopus ...... 600.00 ... 900.00
w/o mouth
Retired

Jabber the parrot .... 15.00 .... 30.00
Born 10/10/97

Jake the mallard .... 10.00 .... 20.00
Born 4/16/97

Jolly the walrus .... 10.00 .... 20.00
Born 12/2/96
Retired

Kiwi the toucan .... 150.00 ... 225.00
Born 9/16/95
Retired

Kuku the cockatoo .... 10.00 .... 20.00
Born 1/5/97

Lefty the donkey .... 225.00 ... 300.00
Born 7/4/96
Retired

Legs the frog .... 15.00 .... 30.00
Born 4/25/93
Retired

Libearty the bear .... 350.00 ... 500.00
Born Summer 1996
Retired

Lizzy the lizard .... 15.00 .... 30.00
Born 5/11/95
Retired

Lizzy the tie-dyed lizard .... 800.00 .. 1250.00
Retired

Lucky the ladybug .... 150.00 ... 250.00
w/7 dots
Retired

Lucky the ladybug .... 10.00 .... 20.00
w/11 dots
Retired

Lucky the ladybug .... 500.00 ... 800.00
w/21 dots
Retired

Magic the dragon .... 35.00 .... 70.00
w/hot pink stitching
Retired

Magic the dragon .... 25.00 .... 45.00
w/light pink stitching
Born 9/5/95
Retired

Manny the manatee .... 140.00 ... 200.00

Born 6/8/95
Retired

Maple the bear . . . . 200.00 . . . 300.00
w/Maple tush tag

Maple the bear . . . . 550.00 . . . 800.00
w/Pride tush tag
Retired

Maple the bear . . . . 400.00 . . . 550.00
w/Special Olympics hang tag
Retired

Mel the koala . . . . 6.00 . . . . 15.00
Born 1/15/96

Mystic the unicorn . . . . 8.00 . . . . 20.00
w/course mane and irides.horn

Mystic the unicorn . . . . 25.00 . . . . 45.00
w/course mane and tan horn
Retired

Mystic the unicorn . . . . 250.00 . . . 425.00
w/fine mane
Retired

Nanook the husky . . . . 6.00 . . . . 12.00
Born 11/21/96

Nip the cat w/pink ears . . . . 600.00 . . . 900.00
Retired

Nip the cat w/white belly . . . 300.00 . . . 500.00
Retired

Nip the cat w/white paws . . . . 12.50 . . . . 25.00
Retired

Nuts the squirrel . . . . 6.00 . . . . 12.00
Born 1/21/96

Patti the purple platypus . . . 10.00 . . . . 20.00
Born 1/6/93
Retired

Patti the raspberry platypus . 700.00 . . 1100.00
Retired

Peace the bear . . . . 20.00 . . . . 50.00
Born 2/1/96

Peanut the lt.blue elephant . . . 12.00 . . . . 20.00
Retired

Peanut the ryl.blue elephant 4000.00 . . 5200.00
Born 1/25/95
Retired

Peking the panda . . . . 1500.00 . . 2200.00
Retired

Pinchers the lobster . . . . 12.00 . . . . 20.00
Born 6/19/93
Retired

Pinky the flamingo . . . . 6.00 . . . 12.00
Born 2/13/95

Pouch the kangaroo . . . . 6.00 . . . 15.00
Born 11/6/96

Pounce the cat . . . . 6.00 . . . 15.00
Born 9/20/97

Prance the cat . . . . 6.00 . . . 15.00
Born 11/20/97

Princess the bear . . . . 100.00 . . . 200.00
PVC tag

Princess the bear . . . . 25.00 . . . 50.00
PE tag

Puffer the puffin . . . . 6.00 . . . 12.00
Born 11/3/97

Pugsley the pug . . . . 6.00 . . . 12.00
Born 5/2/96

Pinchers the lobster . . . . . 4000.00 . . 5000.00
Retired

Quackers the duck . . . . 7.50 . . . 15.00
w/wings
Retired

Quacker(s) the duck . . . . . 2000.00 . . 3000.00
w/o wings
Born 4/19/94
Retired

Radar the bat . . . . 130.00 . . . 200.00
Born 10/30/95
Retired

Rainbow the chameleon . . . . . . 6.00 . . . 15.00
Born 11/14/97

Rex the tyrannosaurus . . . . . 800.00 . . 1200.00
Retired

Righty the elephant . . . . . . 225.00 . . . 300.00
Born 7/4/96
Retired

Ringo the raccoon . . . . 6.00 . . . 12.00
Born 7/14/95

Roary the lion . . . . 6.00 . . . 12.00
Born 2/20/96

Roary the lion . . . . 75.00 . . . 150.00
w/Royals card

Rocket the blue jay . . . . 10.00 . . . 20.00
Born 3/12/97

Rover the dog . . . . 10.00 . . . 20.00
Born 5/30/96
Retired

Scoop the pelican . . . . 6.00 . . . . 12.00
Born 7/1/96

Scottie the terrier . . . . 15.00 . . . . 25.00
Born 6/15/96
Retired

Seamore the seal . . . . 125.00 . . . 200.00
Born 12/14/96
Retired

Seaweed the otter . . . . 6.00 . . . . 15.00
Born 3/19/96

Slither the snake . . . . . . 1600.00 . . 2500.00
Retired

Sly the fox w/brown belly . . . 125.00 . . . 200.00
Retired

Sly the fox w/white belly . . . . . 6.00 . . . . 12.00
Born 9/12/96

Smoochy the frog . . . . 6.00 . . . . 12.00
Born 11/1/97

Snip the cat . . . . 6.00 . . . . 15.00
Born 10/22/96

Snort the bull . . . . 6.00 . . . . 12.00
Born 5/15/95

Snowball the snowman . . . . . 25.00 . . . . 50.00
Born 12/22/96
Retired

Sparky the Dalmatian . . . . . 100.00 . . . 175.00
Born 2/27/96
Retired

Sparky with Dotty tag . . . . . 100.00 . . . 175.00
Retired

Speedy the turtle . . . . 20.00 . . . . 35.00
Born 8/14/94
Retired

Spike the rhinoceros . . . . 6.00 . . . . 12.00
Born 8/13/96

Spinner the spider . . . . 6.00 . . . . 12.00
Born 10/28/96

Splash the whale . . . . 100.00 . . . 150.00
Born 7/8/93
Retired

Spooky the ghost . . . . 25.00 . . . . 40.00
Born 10/31/95
Retired

Spooky the ghost . . . . 350.00 . . . 600.00
w/Spook tag
Retired

Spot the dog w/spot . . . . 40.00 . . . . 70.00
Born 1/3/93
Retired

Spot the dog w/o spot . . . . 1600.00 . . 2500.00
Retired

Spunky the cocker spaniel . . . . 6.00 . . . . 15.00
Born 1/14/97

Squealer the pig . . . . 20.00 . . . . 35.00
Born 4/23/93
Retired

Steg the stegosaurus . . . . . 800.00 . . 1200.00
Retired

Sting the ray . . . . 150.00 . . . 225.00
Born 8/27/95
Retired

Stinger the scorpion . . . . 15.00 . . . . 25.00
Born 9/29/97

Stinky the skunk . . . . 6.00 . . . . 12.00
Born 2/13/95

Stretch the ostrich . . . . 8.00 . . . . 20.00
Born 9/21/97

Stretch the ostrich . . . . 65.00 . . . 125.00
w/St.L. Cards card

Stripes the tiger . . . . 10.00 . . . . 20.00
Black/Caramel
Retired

Stripes the tiger . . . . 250.00 . . . 425.00
Black/Gold
Retired

Stripes the tiger . . . . 550.00 . . . 800.00
Black/Gold w/fuzzy belly
Retired

Stripes the tiger . . . . 65.00 . . . 125.00
w/Tigers card

Strut the rooster . . . . 10.00 . . . . 20.00
Born 3/8/96

Strut the rooster . . . . 125.00 . . . 175.00
w/Pacers card #'d/5000

Tabasco the bull . . . . 150.00 . . . 225.00
Born 5/15/95
Retired

Tank the armadillo w/7 lines . 200.00 . . . 300.00
Retired

Tank the armadillo w/9 lines . 225.00 . . . 300.00
Retired

Tank the armadillo w/shell . . . 50.00 . . . . 80.00

Retired

1997 Teddy	30.00	60.00

Born 12/25/96
Retired

Teddy the brown bear w/New Face	70.00	110.00

Retired

Teddy the brown bear w/Old Face	2700.00	4000.00

Retired

Teddy the cranberry bear w/New Face	1500.00	2200.00

Retired

Teddy the cranberry bear w/Old Face	1500.00	2500.00

Retired

Teddy the jade bear w/New Face	1500.00	2500.00

Retired

Teddy the jade bear w/Old Face	1500.00	2500.00

Retired

Teddy the magenta bear w/New Face	1500.00	2200.00

Retired

Teddy the magenta bear w/Old Face	1500.00	2200.00

Retired

Teddy the teal bear w/New Face	1500.00	2200.00

Retired

Teddy the teal bear w/Old Face	1500.00	2200.00

Retired

Teddy the violet bear w/New Face	1500.00	2200.00

Retired

Teddy the violet bear w/New Face-Employee Tag	3500.00	5000.00

Retired

Teddy the violet bear w/Old Face	1500.00	2200.00

Retired

Tracker the bassett hound	12.50	25.00

Born 6/5/98

Trap the mouse	1200.00	2200.00

Retired

Tuffy the terrier	6.00	12.00

Born 10/12/96

Tusk the walrus	125.00	200.00

Born 9/18/95
Retired

Tusk the walrus w/Tuck tag	125.00	200.00

Retired

Twigs the giraffe	12.00	20.00

Born 5/19/95
Retired

Valentino the bear	10.00	25.00

Born 2/14/94

Valentino the bear w/Yankees card	200.00	350.00

Velvet the panther	18.00	35.00

Born 12/16/95
Retired

Waddle the penguin	12.00	20.00

Born 12/19/95
Retired

Waves the whale	10.00	20.00

Born 12/8/96
Retired

Waves the whale w/Echo tag	15.00	25.00

Retired

Web the spider	1100.00	1800.00

Retired

Weenie the dog	15.00	25.00

Born 7/20/95
Retired

Whisper the deer	15.00	25.00

Born 4/5/97

Wise the owl	30.00	45.00

5/31/97

Wrinkles the dog	6.00	12.00

Born 5/1/96

Ziggy the zebra	12.00	20.00

Born 12/24/95
Retired

Zip the cat w/pink ears	1200.00	2000.00

Retired

Zip the cat w/white belly	350.00	550.00

Retired

Zip the cat w/white paws	30.00	50.00

Retired

Ty Plush Checklists

Many collectors drew a bead on Ty's plush toys long before Beanie Babies made their debut. So for those veteran collectors, and others who have recently ventured beyond the standard beanie realm, we've assembled a checklist of Ty's other popular lines: Attic Treasures, Pillow Pals and Ty Plush.

Attic Treasures, small jointed animals clad in vintage-style clothing, "symbolize the look and feel of eras long ago," describes Ty spokesperson Lori Tomnitz. Pillow Pals are larger, flatter versions of some of the more popular Beanie Babies. They serve as popular gifts for infants. The Ty Plush line includes a variety of quality bears, dogs, monkeys — and more — in all price ranges.

Ty Plush

Name	Color	Size (Inches)	Retired
1991 Collector bear	brown	21	yes
1992 Collector bear	gold	21	yes
1997 Holiday bear	white	14	yes
Ace the Dalmatian	b&w	12	no
Al E. cat	gold	20	no
Al E. cat	gray	20	no
Al E. cat	gold	23	yes
Angel the cat	white	17	no
Angel the cat	white	20	yes
Angel the himalayan cat	white	20	yes
Angora the rabbit	white	11	yes
Angora the rabbit	white	20	yes
Arctic the polar bear	white	12	yes
Arnold the pig (#6001)	pink	20	yes
Arnold the pig (#6001w)	pink	20	yes
Arnold the pig (#6002)	pink	20	yes
Ashes the dog	black	8	yes
Aurora the polar bear	white	13	yes
Baby Buddy the bear	brown	20	yes
Baby Butterball the cat	white	8	yes
Baby Cinnamon the teddy bear	gray	13	yes
Baby Clover the cow	b&w	12	yes
Baby Curly bunny	beige	12	yes
Baby Curly teddy bear	gold	12	not
Baby Curly teddy bear	tan	12	yes
Baby George the gorilla	black	12	no
Baby Ginger the teddy bear	tan	14	no
Baby Lovie the lamb	white	12	yes
Baby Paws the black bear	black	12	no
Baby Paws the bear	sable	12	no
Baby Paws the polar bear	white	12	no
Baby Petunia the pig	pink	12	yes
Baby PJ the teddy bear	sable	12	no
Baby PJ the teddy Bear	white	12	yes
Baby Pokey the rabbit	brown	13	yes
Baby Powder the teddy bear	cream	14	no
Baby Smokey the rabbit	gray	13	yes
Baby Sparky the dalmatian	b&w	20	yes
Baby Spice the teddy bear	gray	13	yes
Bailey the teddy bear	brown	19	yes
Bamboo the panda bear	b&w	13	yes
Bamboo the panda bear	b&w	12	no
Bandit the raccoon	brown	20	yes
Bandit the raccoon	gray	20	yes
Barney the lab	black	20	yes
Baron the teddy bear	brown	18	yes
Beanie the teddy bear	beige	12	yes
Beanie the bunny	beige	12	yes
Beanie the bunny	white	12	yes
Bengal the tiger (sitting)	multi	12	yes
Bengal the tiger (floppy)	multi	12	no
Big Beanie the teddy tear	brown	16	yes
Big Beanie the teddy bear	beige	16	yes
Big Beanie the teddy bear	gold	16	yes
Big Beanie the teddy bear	brown	16	yes
Big Beanie bunny	beige	15	yes
Big Beanie bunny	brown	15	yes
Big Beanie bunny	white	15	yes
Big George the gorilla	black	27	no
Big Jake the monkey	auburn	16	yes
Big Jake the monkey	auburn	unknwn	yes
Big Jake the monkey	chocolate	16	yes
Big Jake the monkey	white	16	yes

TY PLUSH CHECKLIST

Name	Color	Size	Tag
Big Pudgy the Teddy Bear	gray	28	yes
Big Shaggy the Teddy Bear	brown	26	yes
Biscuit the Dog	beige	17	yes
Blackie the Teddy Bear	black	13	yes
Blossom the Rabbit	charcoal	18	yes
Bo the hound Dog	brown&w	20	yes
Boots the Cat	black	16	no
Bows the Rabbit	white	11	no
Brownie the Bear	brown	13	yes
Buckshot the Beagle	multi	20	yes
Buddy the Bear (#5019)	brown	20	yes
Buddy the Bear (#5007)	brown	20	yes
Buster the Dog	gold	unknwn	yes
Butterball the Cat	white	unknwn	yes
Buttercup the Rabbit	gray	18	yes
Buttons the Rabbit	beige	11	no
Candy the Rabbit	white	unknwn	yes
Cha Cha the Monkey	brown	12	no
Charlie the Cocker Spaniel	brown	20	yes
Charlie the Cocker Spaniel (lying)	brown	20	yes
Charlie the Cocker Spaniel (sitting)	brown	20	yes
Chestnut the Squirrel	brown	12	yes
Chi-Chi the Cheetah (#7414)	multi	20	yes
Chi-Chi the Cheetah (#1114)	multi	20	yes
Chips the Dog	brown	12	no
Chuckles the Monkey	brown	15	yes
Churchill the Bull Dog	brown	12	no
Cinders the Dog	black	20	yes
Cinnamon the teddy bear	gold	13	yes
Cinnamon the teddy bear	gray	18	yes
Clover the cow	b&w	20	yes

Name	Color	Size	Tag
Harris the lion (#1115)	brown	20	yes
Honey the dog	brown	20	no
Hooters the owl	brown	9	yes
Hope the teddy bear	gold	10	no
Jake the monkey	brown	unknwn	yes
Jake the monkey	auburn	12	yes
Jake the monkey	auburn	24	yes
Jake the monkey	chocolate	12	yes
Jake the monkey	white	12	yes
Jake the monkey	white	24	yes
Jersey the cow	b&w	20	no
Jersey the cow	bge&w	20	yes
Josh the orangutan	brown	24	yes
Jumbo George the gorilla	black	48	no
Jumbo PJ the teddy bear	sable	40	no
Jumbo PJ the teddy bear	white	40	yes
Jumbo Pumpkin the teddy bear	gray	40	yes
Jumbo Rumples the teddy bear	beige	40	yes
Jumbo Shaggy the teddy bear	beige	40	yes
Jumbo Shaggy the teddy bear	brown	40	yes
Jumbo Shaggy the teddy bear	gold	40	yes
Kasey the koala	brown	13	yes
Kasey the koala	gray	13	yes
Large Curly bunny	beige	24	yes
Large Curly bunny	white	24	yes
Large Curly teddy bear	gold	26	no
Large Curly teddy bear	tan	26	yes
Large Ginger the teddy bear	brown	22	yes
Large Honey the teddy bear	brown	26	yes
Large McGee the teddy bear	brown	26	yes
Large Moonbeam			
Coal the cat	black	16	yes
Cocoa the bear	brown	12	no
Corky the dog	brown	12	no
Cotton the rabbit	white	14	yes
Crystal the cat	white	16	no
Curly the bunny	beige	22	no
Curly the bunny	white	22	no
Curly the teddy bear	gold	18	no
Curly the teddy bear	tan	18	yes
Cuzzy the teddy bear	gray	13	yes
Dakota the dog	gray&white	12	no
Dakota the husky dog	gray	12	yes
Domino the rabbit	b&w	20	yes
Dopey the dog	brown	17	yes
Droopy the dog	brown	15	yes
Dumpling the Teddy Bear	brown	12	yes
Dumpling the teddy bear	white	12	yes
Edmond the teddy bear	gold	21	yes
Eleanor the teddy bear	brown	19	yes
Elmer the elephant	gray	20	yes
Elmer the elephnt (long trnk)	gray	20	yes
Elmer the elephnt (short trnk)	gray	20	yes
Elvis the dog	brown	20	no
Faith the teddy bear	white	10	no
Fido the dog	white	8	yes
Fluffy the cat	white	15	yes
Forest the bear	brown	12	no
Freddie the frog	green	10	yes
Freddie the frog	green	16	no
Frisky the cat	black	17	yes
Fritz the Dalmatian	b&w	20	yes
Fuzzy the teddy bear	gold	13	yes
George the gorilla	black	20	no
Ginger the cat	brown	20	yes
Ginger the teddy bear	brown	18	yes
Ginger the Himalayan cat	brown	20	yes
Harris the lion (#7415)	brown	20	yes

TY PLUSH CHECKLIST

the teddy bear	brown	20	yes
Large Paws the bear	black	28	no
Large Paws the bear	sable	28	no
Large Paws the polar bear	white	28	no
Large Petunia the pig	pink	26	yes
Large Ping Pong the panda	b&w	26	yes
Large PJ the teddy bear	sable	26	no
Large PJ the teddy bear	white	26	yes
Large Powder the teddy bear	cream	22	yes
Large Pudgy the teddy bear	gray	28	yes
Large Pumpkin the teddy bear	gray	26	yes
Large Rumples the teddy bear	beige	26	yes
Large Rumples the teddy bear	gold	26	yes
Large Rusty the dog	rust	26	yes
Large Scruffy the teddy bear	gold	28	yes
Large Scruffy the teddy bear	gold	26	yes
Large Scruffy the teddy bear	cream	26	yes
Large Scruffy the dog	gold	26	yes
Large Shaggy the teddy bear	beige	26	yes
Large Shaggy the teddy bear	brown	26	yes
Large Shaggy the teddy bear	gold	26	yes
Large Snowball the teddy bear	white	26	yes
Large Sparky the Dalmatian	b&w	26	yes
Lazy the bear	gray	20	yes
Leo the lion	brown	22	no

Licorice the cat	black	17	no
Licorice the cat	black	20	yes
Lilly the lamb	white	20	yes
Lovie the lamb	white	20	yes
Lovie the lamb	beige	10	yes
Lovie the lamb	white	20	yes
Lovie the lamb	white	18	yes
Magee the bear	brown	10	no
Maggie the cat (curled)	calico	20	no
Maggie the cat (flat)	calico	20	yes
Mandarin the panda	b&w	13	yes
Mango the orangutan	orange	20	no
Mango the orangutan	white	20	no
Max the dog (#3001)	white	20	yes
Max the dog (#2008)	white	20	yes
McGee the teddy bear	brown	14	yes
McGee the teddy bear	brown	13	yes
Midnight the bear	black	13	yes
Midnight the bear	black	20	yes
Mischief the monkey	brown	unknwn	yes
Mischief the monkey	brown	21	yes
Mischief the monkey (#7000)	auburn	18	yes
Mischief the monkey (#7001)	auburn	18	yes
Mischief the monkey	chocolate	unknwn	yes
Mischief the monkey	chocolate	18	yes
Mischief the monkey ('92-93)	white	18	yes
Mischief the monkey ('88)	white	18	yes
Misty the seal	white	14	yes
Misty the seal	white	11	no
Mittens the cat	gold	12	yes
Mittens the cat	gray	12	yes
Moonbeam the teddy bear	brown	14	yes
Mortimer the moose	brown	18	no

TY PLUSH CHECKLIST

Name	Color	Price	Retired
Muffin the dog	brown	13	no
Nibbles the rabbit	brown	9	no
Nibbles the rabbit	white	9	no
Nutmeg the teddy bear	brown	18	yes
Oreo the panda (lying)	b&w	20	yes
Oreo the panda	b&w	20	yes
Otto the otter	brown	20	yes
Papa PJ the teddy bear	sable	50	no
Papa Pumpkin the teddy bear	gray	50	yes
Papa Rumples the teddy bear	beige	50	yes
Papa Shaggy the teddy bear	beige	50	yes
Papa Shaggy the teddy bear	gold	50	yes
Patches the cat	brown	20	yes
Patches the dog	gold	18	no
Patti the panther	black	20	yes
Paws the bear	black	18	no
Paws the bear	sable	18	no
Paws the polar bear	white	18	no
Peaches the cat	cream	20	yes
Peaches the Himalayan cat	cream	20	yes
Peepers the chick	yellow	9	yes
Pepper the dog	black	12	no
Peter the rabbit	brown	20	yes
Peter the rabbit	brown	14	yes
Petunia the pig	pink	20	yes
Petunia the pig (blue ribbon)	pink	20	yes
Petunia the pig (pink ribbon)	pink	20	yes
Pierre the poodle	white	10	yes
Ping Pong the panda	b&w	13	yes
Ping Pong the panda	b&w	14	yes
PJ the teddy bear	sable	18	no
PJ the teddy bear	white	18	yes
Pokey the rabbit	brown	19	yes
Powder the teddy bear	cream	18	yes
Prayer Bear the teddy bear	gold	14	yes
Prayer Bear the teddy bear	white	14	yes
Pudgy the teddy bear	gray	14	yes
Puffy the cat	gray	15	yes
Pumpkin the teddy bear	gray	18	yes
Rags the teddy bear	beige	12	yes
Rascal the monkey	brown	16	yes
Romeo the teddy bear	white	14	no
Romeo the teddy bear (gld rbbn)	white	14	no
Romeo the teddy bear (M Day)	white	14	no
Rosie the rabbit	gray	20	yes
Ruffles the teddy bear	beige	12	yes
Rufus the teddy bear	beige	18	yes
Rumples the teddy bear	beige	18	yes
Rumples the teddy bear	gold	18	yes
Rusty the dog	rust	20	yes
Sahara the lion ('95-96)	brown	12	yes
Sahara the lion ('98)	brown	12	no
Sam the teddy bear	brown	18	yes
Sarge the German shepherd	brown	20	yes
Scratch the cat	brown	15	yes
Screech the cat	black	15	yes
Scruffy the teddy bear	cream	18	yes
Scruffy the teddy bear	lt gold	18	yes
Scruffy the teddy bear	gold	18	yes
Scruffy the dog	cream	20	yes
Scruffy the dog	gold	20	yes
Scruffy the dog	white	20	yes
Shadow the cat	black	23	yes
Shadow the bear	black	20	yes
Shaggy the teddy bear	beige	18	yes
Shaggy the teddy bear	brown	18	yes
Shaggy the teddy bear	gold	18	yes
Sherlock the			

Name	Color	Size (Inches)	Retired
Basset Hound	brown	12	no
Sherlock the cat	black	20	yes
Shivers the penguin	b&w	9	yes
Silky the cat	black	15	yes
Smokey the rabbit	gray	19	yes
Smokey the cat	gray	20	yes
Smokey the Himalayan cat	gray	18	yes
Sniffles the dog	brown	18	yes
Snowball the teddy bear	white	13	yes
Snowball the teddy bear	white	14	yes
Socks the cat	black	12	yes
Spanky the Saint Bernard	brown	20	yes
Spanky the Cocker Spaniel	brown	8	yes
Sparkles the unicorn	white	20	no
Sparky the Dalmation (#2004)	b&w	20	yes
Sparky the Dalmation (#2012)	b&w	20	yes
Spice the cat	brown	17	no
Spice the teddy bear	gray	18	yes
Spout the elephant (sitting)	gray	9	yes
Spout the elephant (flppy lgs)	gray	9	no
Sugar the teddy bear	white	14	yes
Sugar the polar bear	white	20	yes
Sunny the dog	gold	14	no
Super Arnold the pig	pink	unknwn	yes
Super Buddy the bear	brown	unknwn	yes
Super Chi-Chi the cheetah	multi	52	yes
Super Fritz the Dalmatian	b&w	36	yes
Super George the gorilla	black	36	yes
Super Jake the monkey	white	16	yes
Super Jake the monkey	brown	55	yes
Super Max the dog	white	26	yes
Super Max the dog	white	32	yes
Super Scruffy the teddy bear	brown	28	yes
Super Sparky the Dalmatian	b&w	unkwn	yes
Taffy the dog	brown	12	no
Taffy the dog	brown	8	yes
Tango the orangutan	orange	12	no
Tango the orangutan	white	12	no
Theodore the teddy bear	brown	19	yes
Timber the dog	gray	20	no
Toffee the dog	brown	20	yes
Tulip the pig	pink	18	no
Tumbles the cat	gray	17	yes
Twiggy the giraffe	brown	23	yes
Tygger the tiger (lying)	multi	20	no
Tygger the tiger (standing)	multi	20	yes
Tygger the tiger	white	20	yes
Vanilla the teddy bear	cream	18	yes
Wally the walrus	brown	12	yes
Whinnie the horse	brown	20	yes
Winston the bull dog	brown	20	no
Woolly the lamb	white	9	no
Wuzzy the teddy bear	brown	13	yes
Yappy the Yorkie	brown	8	yes
Yappy the Yorkie	brown	12	no
Yorkie the Yorkie	brown	20	yes
Yukon the bear	black	8	yes
Zulu the zebra	b&w	20	yes

Attic Treasures

Name	Color	Size (Inches)	Retired
Abby the teddy bear	gray	8	yes
Amethyst the cat	white	13	no
Barry the teddy bear	beige	14	yes

TY PLUSH CHECKLIST

Name	Color	Size	Retired
Bearington the teddy bear	brown	14	no
Benjamin the rabbit	brown	9	yes
Bloom the rabbit	white	16	yes
Bluebeary the teddy bear	blue	8	no
Bonnie the chick	yellow	9	no
Boris the teddy bear	black	12	yes
Brewster the dog	rust	12	yes
Carlton the teddy bear	brown	16	yes
Casanova the teddy bear	brown	8	no
Cassie the teddy bear	gray	8	yes
Charles the teddy bear	gray	12	yes
Checkers the panda	b&w	8	no
Chelsea the teddy bear	gold	8	no
Christopher the teddy bear	brown	8	no
Clifford the teddy bear	gold	12	yes
Clyde the teddy bear	brown	12	yes
Cody the teddy bear	brown	8	no
Colby the mouse	brown	11	yes
Copperfield the teddy bear	brown	16	yes
Dexter the teddy bear	brown	9	yes
Dickens the teddy bear	gray	8	no
Digby the teddy bear	brown	12	yes
Domino the panda	b&w	12	yes
Ebony the cat	black	13	no
Ebony the cat	black	15	yes
Emily the teddy bear (1st gen.)	rust	12	yes
Emily the teddy bear (2nd gen.)	rust	12	yes
Emily the teddy bear (w/ hat)	rust	12	yes
Eve the teddy bear	brown	12	no
Fraser the teddy bear	beige	8	no
Frederick the teddy bear	gold	8	yes
Gilbert the teddy bear	gold	8	yes
Gilbert the teddy bear	white	8	yes
Gloria the rabbit	white	12	no
Grace the hippo	gray	12	no
Grady the teddy bear	gold	16	yes
Grant the teddy bear	beige	13	no
Grover the teddy bear	brown	16	yes
Grover the teddy bear	brown	13	yes
Grover the teddy bear	gold	16	yes
Heather the rabbit	white	20	yes
Henry the teddy bear	gold	8	yes
Henry the teddy bear	brown	8	yes
Iris the rabbit	beige	10	no
Ivan the teddy bear	black	8	no
Ivory the cat	white	15	yes
Ivy the rabbit	white	10	no
Jeremy the rabbit	gray	12	yes
Justin the monkey	brown	14	yes
King the frog	green	11	yes
King the frog	green	9	yes
Large Bear the teddy bear	brown	15	no
Lilly the lamb	gray	9	yes
Madison the cow	b&w	10	yes
Malcolm the teddy bear	brown	12	yes
Mason the teddy bear	rust	8	yes
Montgomery the moose	brown	15	no
Morgan the monkey	brown	8	no
Murphy the dog	beige	9	yes
Nicholas the teddy bear	white	8	no
Nola the teddy bear (w/ hat)	white	12	yes
Nola the teddy bear (w/ bow)	white	12	yes
Nola the teddy bear (no bow)	white	12	yes
Oscar the teddy bear	brown	8	yes
Penelope the pig	pink	9	yes
Peppermint the teddy bear	white	8	no
Piccadilly the teddy bear	beige	9	no

Name	Color	Size	Retired
Pouncer the cat	orange	8	yes
Pouncer the cat	orange	8	no
Precious the teddy bear	brown	12	no
Prince the frog	green	8	no
Priscilla the pig	pink	12	yes
Purrcy the cat	black	8	no
Rebecca the teddy bear	brown	12	yes
Rebecca the teddy bear	brown	12	yes
Reggie the teddy bear (red rib.)	gold	8	yes
Reggie the teddy bear (blu rib.)	gold	8	yes
Rose the rabbit	rose	10	no
Samuel the teddy bear	brown	13	no
Sara the rabbit	white	12	yes
Sara the rabbit	white	15	no
Scooter the dog	brown	9	yes
Scotch the teddy bear	brown	14	no
Scruffy the dog	brown	9	no
Shelby the rabbit	gold	9	yes
Sidney the rabbit	gray	15	no
Sire the lion	brown	13	no
Small Bear the teddy bear	beige	9	no
Spencer the dog	beige	15	yes
Squeaky the mouse (no rib.)	brown	8	no
Squeaky the mouse (red rib.)	brown	8	yes
Strawbunny the rabbit	pink	10	no
Tiny Tim the teddy bear	beige	8	yes
Tracey the dog	rust	15	yes
Tulip the rabbit	brown	10	yes
Tyler the teddy bear	beige	12	yes
Watson the teddy bear	lt.pink	14	yes
Wee Willie the teddy bear	brown	8	yes
Whiskers the cat	gray	8	yes
Whiskers the cat (green ear)	gray	8	no
Woolie the teddy bear	gold	12	yes
Woolie the teddy bear	brown	12	yes

Pillow Pals

(All Pillow Pals 15 inches, unless noted otherwise)

Name	Color	Retired
BaBa the lamb (21 in.)	white	no
Bruiser the bulldog	brown&white	no
Carrots the rabbit	pink	no
Clover the rabbit	white	no
Foxy the fox	brown&white	no
Glide the dolphin	blue&white	no
Huggy the bear	blue	yes
Huggy the bear	blue	yes
Meow the cat	tan	no
Meow the cat	gray	yes
Moo the cow	b&w	no
Oink the pig	pink	no
Paddles the platypus	fuschia	no
Purr the tiger	yellow&orange	yes
Red the bull	red&beige	no
Ribbit the frog	yellow/green	no
Ribbit the frog	green	yes
Sherbet the teddy bear	tie dye	no
Snap the turtle	yellow	yes
Snap the turtle	green/yellow	yes
Snuggy the bear	pink	yes
Snuggy the bear	pink	yes
Speckles the leopard	multi	yes
Spotty the Dalmatian	b&w	no
Squirt the elephant	blue	no
Swinger the monkey	brown	no
Tide the whale	b&w	no
Tubby the hippo	lavender	no
Woof the dog	brown	no
Zulu the zebra (thin stripes)	pink&green	yes
Zulu the zebra (thick stripes)	pink&green	yes

Teenie Beanie Baby Introduction

McDonald's spokesmen were the first to admit that they weren't prepared for the onslaught of collectors during the initial Teenie Beanie Babies promotion in April 1997. After producing 100 million of the animal toys, the fast food chain planned to give away a beanie with each Happy Meal during a five-week campaign. Less than two weeks later, supplies were depleted.

McDonald's was a bit more prepared in '98, upping its selection from 10 Teenies to 12 and allowing customers to purchase the toys with food orders other than Happy Meals. But collectors still snatched up all Teenies long before the program was scheduled to conclude.

Collectors expect the promotion to continue in 1999.

TEENIE BEANIE BABIES

Teenie Beanie Babies have been known to confuse collectors. Many collectors have unfairly blamed the Teenie Beanie Babies for the scarcity of Ty Beanie Babies on the market the past two summers, but Ty merely sold a licensing agreement to McDonald's and didn't actually produce the non-plush toys.

Nevertheless, the Teenie Beanie Babies are good representations of their larger Ty counterparts.

1997 McDonald's Teenie Beanie Babies

Chocolate
Chops
Goldie
Lizz
Patti
Pinky
Quacks
Seamore
Snort
Speedy

TEENIE BEANIE BABIES

TEENIE BEANIE BABIES

1998 McDonald's Teenie Beanie Babies

Bones
Bongo
Doby
Happy
Inch
Mel
Peanut
Pinchers
Scoop
Twigs
Waddle
Zip

Disney Introduction

By Dustie Meads

DISNEY INTRODUCTION

It's just a pile of plastic pellets, polyester fiber and cloth. Individually, they don't seem too exciting.

But sew them together, toss in a little history, a friendly price point and the most familiar characters on the planet and you get the Disney Mini Bean Bag Plush — commonly known as Disney Beanies — one of the fastest growing and most popular collectible toy lines on the market.

Introduced in 1997, the Disney Mini Bean Bags have enjoyed immense popularity among beanie collectors and Disney enthusiasts, and are second only to Ty Inc.'s Beanie Babies in beanie popularity.

Indeed, it wasn't until Disney began to release their Bean Bag characters that any other beanie toy seriously challenged Ty's undisputed dominance of the beanie market. Already Disney has released more than 125 different Mini Bean Bags in its line, retiring some and labeling others as limited edition beanies. In short, Disney is playing the game the way collectors want it to be played. And Disney is doing it with established popular characters such as Mickey Mouse, Winnie the Pooh and Flubber.

"I found that the interest in them is much greater than I expected," beanie collector and dealer Sheri Gazwan of Illinois, Mo., said in a recent interview

DISNEY INTRODUCTION

for *Beckett Hot Toys*. "They're fun to find and people's interest in them have made them ardent collectors."

Not bad for a line of toys Disney first introduced as a "test."

That test came in May 1997, when Disney sent its first beanie efforts to exclusively owned Disney Stores. The original test characters — Pluto, Goofy, Eeyore, Piglet, Tigger, a 101 Dalmatian, Sebastian and Flounder from The Little Mermaid, and two of the seven Dwarfs (Grumpy and Dopey) — were sent to 30 stores to gauge market interest for another beanie toy.

Toward the end of the test period, Disney Stores introduced a 9-inch Mickey and Minnie Mouse set to the group, bringing the test set total to 13.

Very few changes were made to the characters during the test period that ran through September 1997. The test proved a huge success, and Disney began manufacturing the Mini Bean Bag Plush characters for larger distribution through its theme parks (both stateside and abroad), catalog, two Club Disney locations in California (fun centers for children and their parents) and, of course, Disney Stores.

Most of the test characters underwent complete design changes when the collection was introduced to the remaining Disney Stores in the U.S.

Since then, some of the other characters have undergone a number of changes — some large, some very minor — but not even the slightest alterations have gone unnoticed.

Collectors use the Internet to exchange updates on variations, release dates, shipment shortages and retirement announcements.

Collectors, in turn, flood Disney Stores and pepper the Cast Members (Disney's term for store employees) with questions like:
How many boxes did you get? Do you expect another shipment?
Which characters are you running short of?

DISNEY INTRODUCTION

Collectors have discovered that the availability of Disney beanies isn't problematic. Sure, some sell out the day they're introduced. But Disney usually restocks characters and quickly makes that beanie available at most of the Disney Stores.

There are exceptions, of course. The Flubber sound bean bag appeared only at select Disney Stores and sold out in minutes, and the Christopher Robin bean bag and the "Alice in Wonderland" collection of eight beanies also did not make it to every Disney Store shelf.

However, most of the characters do reach each Disney Store. Better yet for collectors, many Disney Stores feature mail order departments, so it's not necessary to live near a Disney Store or theme park to collect the beanies. That simple access alone has added a great deal to the appeal of the Disney beanie line.

The boom in Disney beanies certainly can be seen on the secondary market where some retired characters and harder-to-find pieces are commanding top prices.

In December '97, Disney introduced special, limited edition characters for the Christmas holiday season and announced the first five retirees. As those bean bags disappeared from the stores, collectors were left to turn to the secondary market. Soon thereafter, prices on the secondary market began to reflect the law of supply and demand. The higher the prices went up, the more demand for specific beanies increased.

Check out any beanie show, and you're likely to see Disney beanies on the tables. The Internet has also contributed greatly to the growth of the line. Hundreds of secondary "store fronts" have popped up on the Web, with collectors buying, selling and trading Disney beanies. Just like with Ty's Beanie Babies, most Disney collectors want Mint tags (either Disney Store, Walt Disney World or Mouseketoys).

The ranks of Disney Mini Bean Bag Plush is, indeed, growing. So much so that Disney instituted what's known in collecting circles as "The 2 p.m. Rule": Employees do not put out new Beanies, nor field phone calls on the new characters, until 2 p.m. the day they arrive. If a shipment arrives after 2 p.m., they are put out at 2 p.m. the next day. Disney also has added a two-character limit on the new issues for the first day of availability, but allows collectors to purchase as many as they wish after the first day of release.

DISNEY INTRODUCTION

Abu

Released June 1998.

Description Monkey from the movie Aladdin.

Availability As easy to find as they come, swinging from the shelves at Walt Disney World, Disney Stores and Club Disney.

Value History Unchanged.

Alien

Released December 1997.

Description Three-eyed Alien from the movie Toy Story.

Availability Alien and the other Toy Story characters are available at Disney Stores.

Value History Unchanged.

Bagherra

Released March 1998.

Description Black Panther who helps Moogli in The Jungle Book. Some of the first Bagherras released featured misspellings on the tush tags.

Availability Currently available at Disney Stores.

Value History The Bagherras with the erred tush tags are worth twice as much as current value.

DISNEY SECTION

158

Baloo

Released March 1998.

Description This large friendly bear befriends Moogli in The Jungle Book.

Availability A bear necessity for any collection, Baloo is currently in stock at Disney Stores.

Value History Unchanged.

Bambi

Released September 1997.

Retired June 11, 1998.

Description Does Bambi, the darling of Disney's classic animated tale, really need a description?

Availability Despite retirement, Bambi still can be hunted at the theme parks and many Disney Stores.

Value History Bambi already has doubled in value after retirement, and as he becomes harder to find at retail level, look for his value to climb.

BEN ALI GATOR

Released May 1998.

Description Dancing alligator from the Disney classic Fantasia.

Availability Ali is still available at Disney Stores, and can be ordered as part of the Fantasia set from Disneyland.

Value History Unchanged. However, his tag identifies him as Croc, and collectors suspect the tag soon will be changed, leading to an increase in value.

DISNEY SECTION

DISNEY SECTION

Black Card Man

Released May 1998.

Description One of the card men soldiers of the Queen of Hearts in Alice in Wonderland.

Availability The whole Alice in Wonderland set came to select stores and disappeared quickly. They have not been seen since and speculation is that this set was a test of districts. They have not been retired or considered limited, so they may be back in stores soon.

Value History During their absence Black Card Man and his friends are commanding a secondary market price of $20 to $25 apiece and up to $125 for the complete set of eight characters.

Brer Bear

Released April 1998.

Description Bear character from Song of the South.

Availability A semi-rare Brer Bear only available at the theme parks.

Value History Value on this toy and the Song of the South set fluctuates with availability. When the theme parks are sold out, the set of four sells for as much as $75.

Brer Fox

Released April 1998.

Description Fox character from Song of the South.

Availability Better check the theme parks.

Value History When available in the parks for mail order, value for the set drops to about $50.

DISNEY SECTION

BRER RABBIT

Released April 1998.
Description Character from Song of the South.
Availability Fluctuates; hare today and gone tomorrow.
Value History Brer Rabbit's value depends on availability.

Buzz Lightyear

Released December 1997.

Description The space man from Toy Story comes in two versions. The first version includes kneepads and an upside down "V" on the vest.

Availability The second version Buzz is as close as the nearest Disney Store.

Value History First version Buzz is worth twice as much as his current release.

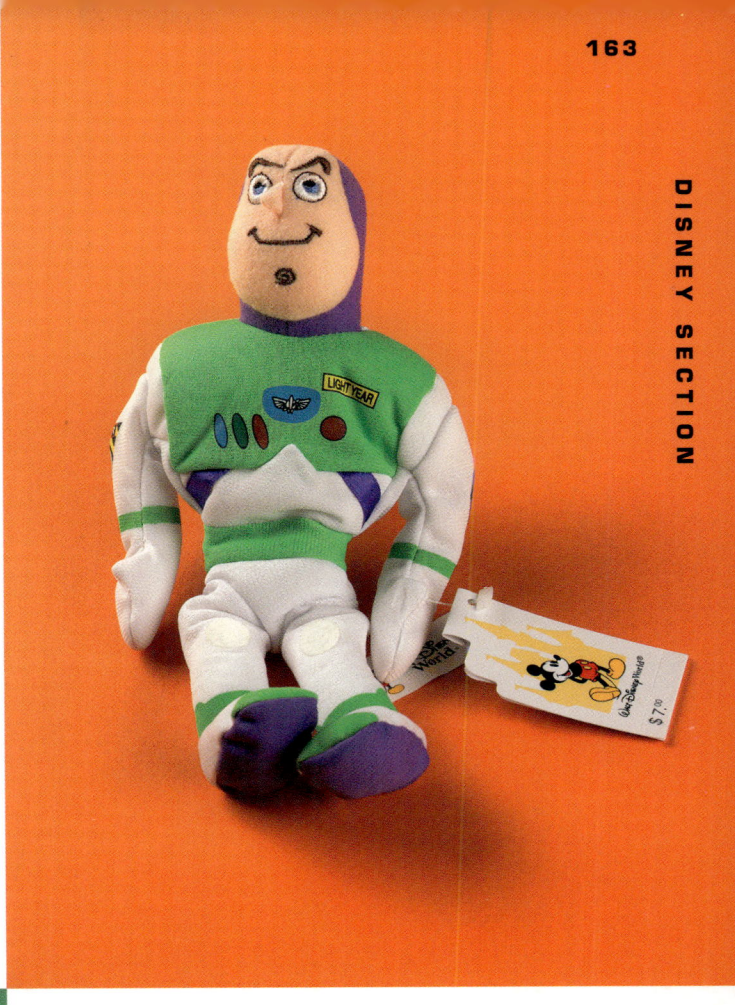

Captain Hook

Released February 1998.

Description The ruthless pirate captain who tries to capture Peter in Peter Pan.

Availability Hook's currently available at Disney Stores.

Value History Unchanged.

DISNEY SECTION

Cheshire Cat

Released May 1998.

Description The grinning, disappearing cat from Alice in Wonderland.

Availability Cheshire, along with the others in the Alice in Wonderland set, made a quick disappearing act after showing up in select stores. They have not been seen since, and there is speculation that this set was a test of districts. They have not been retired or are considered limited beanies and may return to stores.

Value History Cheshire and the others can be found for $20 to $25, at least until they reappear on Disney Store shelves.

Christopher Robin

Released June 1998.

Description The boy who befriends Pooh and Friends in the 100 Acre Wood.

Availability For now, Christopher is an easy find at Disney Stores.

Value History After his first release, he became scarce and his value surged. But Christopher eventually was restocked, bringing his value back to the current retail level.

Chip

Released March 1998.

Description This fast-talking Chipmunk from the Chip and Dale cartoons has his name embroidered on his footpad.

Availability Chip and Dale are both available at most Disney Stores.

Value History Some error beanies with no name or the wrong name (Chip appears on Dale's foot and vice versa) are worth double or triple the current releases.

Cricket

Released June 1998.

Description The little "lucky" Cricket from the newest Disney animated movie Mulan.

Availability There's no luck required in finding this guy at Disney Stores.

Value History Unchanged, but should Disney decide to fix Cricket's tag to reflect his actual name of Cri Kee, his value is sure to increase.

CROCK

Released February 1998.

Description The crocodile in Peter Pan that ate Captain Hook's hand. Crock is sometimes referred to as Tic Tock, because he swallowed a clock and could be heard whenever he was near the boat.

Availability You won't have to give your right arm for this one. Just go to your local Disney Store.

Value History Unchanged.

DAISY DUCK

Released December 1977.

Description Donald Duck's girlfriend from the classic animated cartoons comes in regular and theme park (more plush and with plastic eyes) versions.

Availability No trouble finding Daisy at the theme parks, Disney Stores or through the catalog.

Value History The theme park version of Daisy sometimes commands double the current retail value of other Daisy bean bags.

Dale

Released March 1998.

Description This cute little chipmunk has his name embroidered on his footpad to avoid confusion. But so much for clarity; Dale has been found with Chip's name on some beanies.

Availability Currently easy to acquire at most Disney Stores.

Value History Erred Dale is worth double or triple the value of a current, corrected Dale.

Dewey

Released   March 1998.

Description   One of Donald Duck's three trouble-prone nephews, Dewey debuted with his brothers wearing the wrong color before being re-released in his trademark blue from the Duck Tail cartoons. His Walt Disney World version is more plush and larger.

Availability   Available at Walt Disney World and Disney Stores.

Value History   The original error sets sell for more than the current sets, but prices have fluctuated. They appear to be stabilizing at about $50 for the set.

Donald Duck

Released   September 1997.

Description   Donald is sometimes considered one of the original test beanies, because he entered the market right on the tail end of the test and then quickly underwent a bit of a style change. There is also a Walt Disney World Donald that is more plush.

Availability   Showing no signs of an early retirement, Donald can be purchased at Disney Stores, Walt Disney World and through the catalog.

Value History   Unchanged for the current version. The "test" version, with larger collar and tuck in his hat, sells for about $12 to $16.

Tomorrow Land Donald

Released May 1998.

Description Donald is dressed in a silver space suit as part of the Tomorrow Land Collection of the Fab Five (Donald, Mickey, Minnie, Pluto and Goofy).

Availability Tomorrow Land Donald can be found at Disneyland and through the catalog and could be coming to Disney Stores soon.

Value History Before this set was available through the catalog, sets sold for as much as $75. Since the addition theme park mail order and rumors of a Disney Store appearance, prices have dropped significantly.

Duchess

Released March 1998.

Description The beautiful white mother cat with a proud stance and gold collar from the animated movie The Aristocats comes in two versions (the first version sports black whiskers).

Availability The first version is a tough one to find; version two is a Disney Store and catalog regular.

Value History The first version Duchess, with whiskers, has risen in value to $15-$25.

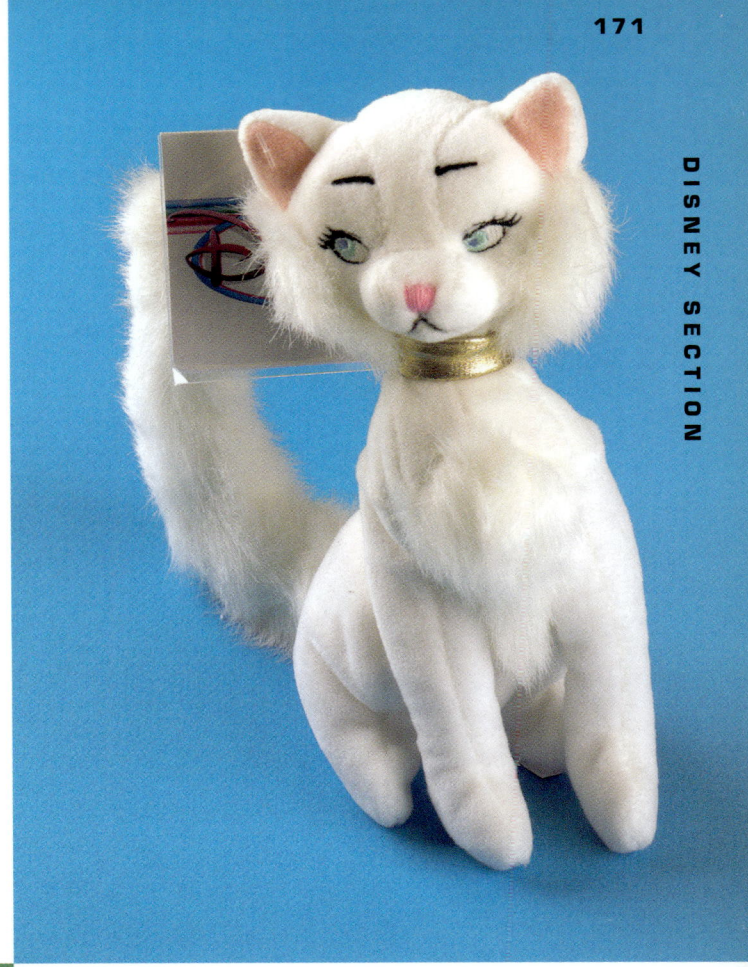

Dumbo

Released January 1998.

Description There are three distinct variations of this big-eared elephant: The Disney Store Dumbo has a pink and orange collar, the theme park Dumbo wears an orange collar and a felt feather in his trunk, and the catalog Dumbo sports a pink and blue collar and a felt feather in his trunk.

Availability Even the laziest collectors should be able to procure at least one version of this toy.

Value History When the Dumbo with the felt feather first came out, prices climbed. But supply eventually met demand, dropping Dumbo's price to the current retail value.

DISNEY SECTION

Eeyore

Released September 1997.

Description The little blue (in more ways than one) donkey who is a friend of Winnie the Pooh was one of the original test beanies. He underwent a variation change into the current Eeyore, but the differences were slight (larger size and less beans). There is also a gray version available from the theme parks.

Availability Theme Parks, catalog and Disney Stores all carry Eeyore.

Value History Gray Eeyore has fetched from $15 to $25, while other Eeyores remain at retail price.

Classic Eeyore

Released December 1977.

Description This lighter blue Eeyore was designed with more of a old-fashioned look in mind.

Availability He's an easy find at Disney Stores and through the catalog.

Value History Unchanged.

Christmas Eeyore

Released October 1977.

Description This Eeyore, wearing a pair of reindeer antlers, was released as a limited edition holiday toy.

Availability He's still available at some stores, but Eeyore is becoming increasingly harder to find.

Value History As Eeyore continues to disappear from stores his value will go up. He's presently valued at $15 to $25.

DISNEY SECTION

FIGARO

Released January 1998.
Description Black kitten from Pinocchio.
Availability Easy to find at Disney Stores and through the catalog.
Value History Unchanged.

Flubber

Released November 1997.

Retired December 22, 1997.

Description Little giggly green guy from the movie with the same name.

Availability He's a tough find on the secondary market.

Value History Shortly after Flubber's retirement, the smiling toy began to climb in value, reaching $30 to $40.

Sound Flubber

Released April 1998.

Description Same as regular Flubber, save for the imbedded sound box that allows him to make sounds when shaken.

Availability Although not officially retired, Sound Flubber was unavailable in stores by mid-summer 1998. He first came to select stores in limited quantity, and his price reflected his scarcity. After a month, he reappeared in limited numbers at Disneyland, and then reappeared again in the catalog. Collectors suspect he'll make future appearances (Club Disney, perhaps?), but he's a rare find until then.

Value History Flubber has sold from as high as $100 to as low as $15. His current value is about $20-$30.
Released: September 1997.

FAB SIX

Released Unknown.

Description These theme park beanies are a variation of their Disney Store counterparts (the Fab Five). They're more plush, more plump and display plastic eyes. The Fab Six also includes Daisy, and, unlike the Disney Store version, the theme park Mickey and Minnie are not retired.

Availability The Fab Six can be ordered from both Walt Disney World and Disneyland.

Value History Common and current.

DISNEY SECTION

FLOUNDER

Released September 1997.

Retired Dec. 22, 1997.

Description Chubby little fish friend of Ariel in The Little Mermaid.

Availability Flounder is still a staple at Disney Stores and theme parks and through Club Disney and the catalog despite retired status.

Value History Due to a very large school of Flounders, retirement has done nothing to change the toy's value.

Flower

Released September 1997.

Retired June 11, 1998.

Description Shy skunk friend of Bambi from the movie Bambi.

Availability Still can be found at the theme parks, Disney Stores and through the catalog.

Value Histry Still unchanged, but as Flower becomes more scarce at the stores, expect her value to rise.

Figment

Released May 1997.

Description Figment is a Walt Disney World exclusive and mascot for Walt Disney World Theme Park, Epcot.

Availability Becoming increasingly harder to find.

Value History Values have climbed to as much as $35 after Figment performed a disappearing act at the theme parks.

Geppetto

Released January 1998.

Description Pinocchio's woodcarving adopted father in Pinocchio, sans glasses. The toy originally was designed to have glasses, but it's not likely any Gepettos with specs made it past Disney's safety inspection.

Availability Disney Stores, catalog.

Value History Unchanged.

GENIE

Released June 1998.

Description The blue wise-cracking Genie from the movie Aladdin.

Availability This new release may be found at Disney Stores, Walt Disney World and Club Disney.

Value History Unchanged.

GOPHER

Released June 1998.

Description A friend of Winnie the Pooh.

Availability Disney Stores, catalog.

Value History Unchanged.

DISNEY SECTION

Goofy

Released September 1997.

Description The friend of Mick has both theme park and Disney Store variations. The theme park Goofy is more plush, is stuffed with more pellets and has plastic eyes.

Availability From Disney Stores, to the catalog to the theme parks, Goofy is plentiful.

Value History Unchanged.

Tomorrow Land Goofy

Released May 1998.

Description Goofy is part of the Tomorrow Land Collection of the Fab Five (along with Donald, Mickey, Minnie and Pluto).

Availability He can be found at Disneyland and through the catalog.

Value History With availability for this set limited to Disneyland, Goofy and Co. were originally selling for $65 to $75. But if the set eventually makes its way to stores, the value will likely drop to retail.

Gus Mouse

Released April 1998.

Description The fat little mouse from the movie Cinderella.

Availability Gus still can be ordered through the catalog and Disney Stores.

Value History Unchanged.

DISNEY SECTION

DISNEY SECTION

Huey

Released March 1998.

Description One of Donald Duck's three nephews, Huey has undergone several changes after having his name tag misspelled (Hewey) on the Disney Store set and debuting in the wrong color.

Availability Huey and his brothers Dewey and Louie are available at Walt Disney World and Disney Stores.

Value History Original error sets of all three nephews have sold for more than the current sets, fluctuating before recently stabilizing at about $50.

Herbie

Released May 1998.

Description The high-flying, side-splitting Volkswagon from the movie The Love Bug.

Availability Plentiful at Disney Stores and Club Disney.

Value History Unchanged.

Hyacinth Hippo

Released May 1998.

Description The Dancing Hippo from Walt Disney Classic Fantasia.

Availability Hippo is at Disney Stores and at Disneyland as part of the Fantasia set.

Value History Unchanged.

Iago

Released June 1998.

Description Red Parrot from the movie Aladdin.

Availability Iago can be found at Disney Stores.

Value History Unchanged.

Jaq Mouse

Released April 1998.

Description Friend of Gus Mouse from the movie Cinderella.

Availability Jaq and Gus are at all Disney Stores.

Value History Unchanged.

DISNEY SECTION

Jewel

Released September 1997.

Retired Dec. 1997.

Description One of the puppies from the movie 101 Dalmatians.

Availability Disneyland may be your best bet; Jewel is becoming increasingly hard to find at Disney Stores.

Value History Jewel's price is beginning to rise as availability decreases. Her current value is $15-$20.

Kiara

Released June 1998.

Description Lion Cub from new Disney movie Simba's Pride.

Availability Kiara can be bought at both Disney Stores and Disneyland.

Value History Unchanged.

Jock

Released June 1998.

Description This furry canine from Lady and the Tramp is hard to overlook, even on crowded Disney Store shelves.

Availability Jock wasn't caught up in the rumors surrounding other summer '98 releases and has been abundant.

Value History Unchanged. Jock is available at the retail price.

Jiminy Cricket

Released January 1998.

Description Cricket who befriends Pinocchio in the Move Pinocchio.

Availability An easy find at Disney Stores.

Value History Unchanged.

DISNEY SECTION

DISNEY SECTION

190

Kovu

Description Lion Cub from new Disney movie Simba's Pride.

Availability Disney Stores and Disneyland carry Kovu.

Value History Unchanged.

Kanga

Released February 1998.

Description Kangaroo mother and friend of Winnie the Pooh doesn't have Roo in this edition.

Availability Kanga is an easy find at Disney Stores and theme parks.

Value History Unchanged.

King Louie

Released: March 1998.

Description: Orangutan from the movie The Jungle Book.

Availability: Look no further than Disney Stores.

Value History: Unchanged.

DISNEY SECTION

192

LITTLE BROTHER

Released May 1998.

Description Darling dog from the movie Mulan.

Availability Little Brother is sure to make a longer appearance at Disney Stores and the theme parks than he did in the movie.

Value History Unchanged.

LADY

Released December 1997.

Description Cocker Spaniel from the classic film Lady and the Tramp.

Availability Appearing with Tramp at Disney Stores.

Value History Unchanged.

Lucky

Released September 1997.

Description Puppy from the classic 101 Dalmatians.

Availability Easy to find at all Disney Stores.

Value History Unchanged.

DISNEY SECTION

LOUIE

Released March 1998.

Description One of Donald Duck's three mischievous nephews and recurring standout in the Duck Tails cartoons. Like his brothers Dewey and Huey, Louie underwent a change in color to his current green.

Availability Available at Walt Disney World and Disney Stores.

Value History Current sets sell for retail, but original error sets of all three nephews sell for about $50.

MARIE

Released March 1998.

Description The white kitten and daughter of Duchess from the movie The Aristocats comes in seven-inch and eight-inch versions, but variations are slight.

Availability Can be ordered from Disney Stores and the catalog.

Value History Unchanged.

Mad Hatter

Released May 1997.

Description Crazy Mad Hatter from the tea party in the animated tale Alice in Wonderland.

Availability This toy could only be found on the secondary market during the summer of '98 but has been rumored to be making a return to Disney Stores.

Value History Because the whole Alice in Wonderland set came to just certain stores and disappeared quickly, the Alice beanies are in high demand, fetching more than $25 per character.

DISNEY SECTION

MERLIN

Released March 1998.

Description Wizard character was released as a Club Disney Exclusive.

Availability Merlin can be hard to find at either of the two Club Disney locations.

Value History This guy, depending on availability, is all over the board. Currently, Merlin can be purchased for $20-$25 on the secondary market.

MICKEY MOUSE

Released September 1997.

Retired June 1998.

Description The one who started it all.

Availability Some Disney Stores still carry Mick, but supplies are running out.

Value History Mickey appears headed for a secondary market surge.

Graduation/Grad Nite Mickey

Released May 1998.

Description There are two versions, both wearing cap and gowns, of the limited edition beanie for the Grad Nite ceremonies at the theme parks. The Walt Disney World version also wears Bermuda Shorts under his gown, but the majority of Walt Disney World Grad Mickeys lack yellow ribbons on their diplomas.

Availability He's a tough one to find.

Value History Graduation Mickey has shown a steady increase and is usually packaged with Graduation Pooh. Set prices start at about $45.

Sorcerer Mickey

Released May 1998.

Description This Mickey, wearing his sorcerer outfit from the animated classic Fantasia, is a favorite for many Disney collectors.

Availability He still can be found at Disney Stores and Disneyland.

Value History Unchanged.

Santa Mickey

Released October 1997.

Description This limited edition Mickey is wearing a Santa outfit and hat.

Availability Still available at some stores, but he's becoming harder to find.

Value History Because of the large quantity of this toy, it's value hasn't changed much to date.

Pilot Mickey

Released July 1998.

Description This version of Mickey, complete with cap and goggles and jacket, was a summer release along with Tourist Mickey, Liberty Minnie and (unavailable for this edition) Pilot Pooh and Hula Minnie.

Availability Rumors that Pilot Mickey was highly limited upon release sent collectors scrambling, but he quickly made an appearance in the catalog and began showing up in greater numbers at the Disney Store.

Value History Pilot Mickey is current, now that collectors are sure of his abundance.

Tomorrow Land Mickey

Released May 1998.

Description Mickey joins Fab Five members Donald, Minnie, Pluto and Goofy for this release.

Availability Mickey and friends can be found at Disneyland and in the catalog. Look for a possible future appearance in stores.

Value History Trading has dropped from $65-$75 a set as collectors wait for the Tomorrow Land characters to resurface in Disney Stores.

Valentine Mickey

Released January 1998.

Description Mickey carries a red satin heart in this limited edition holiday beanie.

Availability He can only be found on the secondary market.

Value History Was unchanged while supply lasted, but prices for Valentine Mickey have steadily increased.

Tourist Mickey

Released July 1998.

Description Mickey, with his multi-colored shirt, hat and camera, would blend in well with the millions of tourists who visit Disneyland and Walt Disney World each year.

Availability Tourist Mickey, just like Pilot Mickey and the other July 1998 releases (Liberty Minnie, Pilot Pooh and Hula Minnie) wasn't as scarce as collectors originally believed. He can be purchased at the Disney Store or through the catalog.

Value History Retail, assuming you didn't get caught up in the hoopla surrounding his release.

Minnie Mouse

Released September 1997.

Retired June 1998.

Description Mickey's love interest wears a red and white polka dot dress with a large bow to match. This version is not to be confused with the non-retired theme parks version.

Availability She's becoming harder to find at Disney Stores, but the theme park Minnie remains in circulation.

Value History We will see her gradually going up in value as supply dwindles.

Liberty Minnie

Released July 1998.

Description Torch-bearing Liberty Minnie, meticulously designed, should satisfy both patriotic and nit-picking collectors. She was released along with Pilot Mickey, Tourist Mickey and Pilot Pooh and Hula Minnie.

Availability Liberty and her fellow July releases are now easy to find at the Disney Store and through the catalog.

Value History Liberty is current, now that there are plenty of her to go around.

Mrs. Santa Minnie

Released October 1997.

Description Minnie's limited edition beanie sports a Santa outfit with white frilly bloomers and Santa hat.

Availability Like many of the other holiday beanies, Minnie still can be found in some stores.

Value History Because of the numbers of this Minnie released, the value has remained pretty close to retail.

Tomorrow Land Minnie

Released May 1998.

Description Minnie teams up with the rest of the Fab Five for this outer space line.

Availability There's always Disneyland and the catalog.

Value History Theme park mail order and rumors of Disney Store release have pushed the value of this beanie back to retail level.

Valentine Minnie

Released January 1998.

Description Minnie's red dress and bow are adorned with white hearts instead of polka dots for this limited holiday release.

Availability Forget about finding Minnie in the stores.

Value History Minnie is on the rise while supply shrinks.

Mr. Smee

Released March 1998.

Description Captain Hook's sidekick from the tale Peter Pan.

Availability Good. Mr. Smee is as close as your local Disney Store.

Value History Unchanged.

Sound Mu-Shu

Released May 1998.

Description This dragon from Mulan brags to those who bump him that he is "the powerful, the pleasurable, the indestructible Mu-Shu."

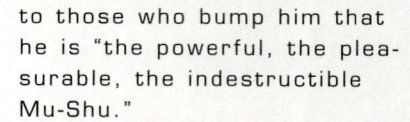

Availability Mu-Shu is still a Disney Store selection.

Value History Unchanged.

Nala

Released January 1998.

Description Female lion cub from The Lion King.

Availability Nala is at Disney Stores, Walt Disney World and in the catalog.

Value History Unchanged.

Nana

Released February 1998.

Description Large nurse maid dog from the movie Peter Pan.

Availability Check Disney Stores or the catalog.

Value History Unchanged.

DISNEY SECTION

OWL

Released February 1998.

Description Wise old owl friend of Winnie the Pooh.

Availability Spreading wisdom at Disney Stores and theme parks.

Value History Unchanged.

PAIN

Released December 1997.

Description This little purple character is a special edition beanie given as a gift with the advance purchase of the video version of Hercules at Disney Stores. Leftovers were tagged and sold but now can only be found through the secondary market.

Value History Value was high until Pain was tagged and sold. Now the price is climbing again.

Panic

Released December 1997.

Retired Limited Special Edition.

Description This little green character from Hercules teamed with Pain for Disney's recent video promotion. Panic also found its way onto shelves once the promotion was over.

Availability Fellow collectors are the only sources for finding Panic.

Value History After a brief dip, Panic's value is back on the upswing.

DISNEY SECTION

Pegasus

Released September 1997.
Retired December 1997.
Description Flying mythological horse from Hercules.
Availability Theme parks and Disney Stores are sold out.
Value History Pegasus' value has steadily increased.

Peter Pan

Released February 1998.
Description The boy who didn't want to grow up.
Availability There's plenty of Peter Pans at Disney Stores.
Value History Unchanged.

PIGLETT

Released September 1997.

Description Insecure friend of Winnie the Pooh.

Availability Piglett may be found at Disney Stores and the theme parks.

Value History Unchanged.

CLASSIC PIGLETT

Released December 1997.

Description Call it a toned-down version of the original: softer colors and edges.

Availability He's at Disney Stores.

Value History Unchanged.

Pluto

Released September 1997.

Description The Mouse's best friend comes in Disney Store and theme park versions (the theme park version is larger).

Availability You shouldn't have any problem finding this faithful dog.

Value History Unchanged.

Christmas Pluto

Released October 1997.

Description Pluto follows Eeyore's lead, sporting antlers for this holiday theme park release.

Availability A pretty hard find; might try the Internet.

Value History Pluto's value has steadily risen since Christmas '97. His present value ranges from $25-$35.

Tomorrow Land Pluto

Released May 1998.

Description Another of the Fab Five for theme park release.

Availability Pluto can be found at Disneyland and in the catalog, and a Disney Store release could follow.

Value History Pluto and the rest of the Tomorrow Land group may never reach their previous high of $65-$75 a set, when their availability was limited to Disneyland.

DISNEY SECTION

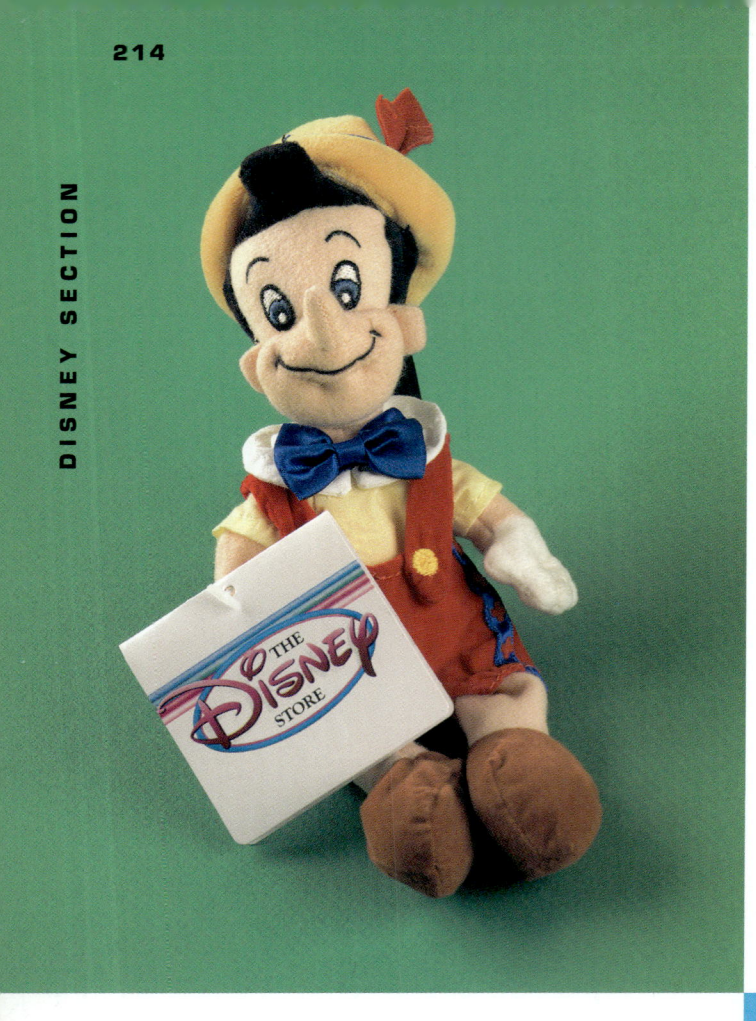

Pinocchio

Released January 1998.

Description The little wooden boy who wished upon a star.

Availability With no retirement in sight, Pinocchio should be hanging around Disney Stores for a while.

Value History Unchanged.

Pooh

Released September 1997.

Description The endearing bear who lives in the 100 Acres Wood with his friends.

Availability Disney Stores and the theme parks can accommodate Pooh lovers.

Value History Unchanged.

BUMBLE BEE POOH

Released April 1998.

Description Pooh donning a bee costume makes for quite possibly the most eye-catching beanie on the planet.

Availability Disney Stores and the theme parks usually have Pooh in stock, but because of the bear's popularity, he can often be hard to find.

Value History Expect to pay from retail to $15, depending on availability.

DISNEY SECTION

Christmas Pooh

Released October 1997.

Description Pooh dons a Santa cap in this limited edition bean bag. The theme park version includes a green scarf.

Availability Once Walt Disney World runs out, Pooh will become hard find.

Value History Prices are now beginning to climb as supply shrinks.

Easter Pooh

Released February 1998.

Description This limited holiday edition toy shows Pooh dressed in a lavender Easter Bunny suit.

Availability Expect to have to hunt for this one.

Value History His price has been rising quickly to as much as $85.

Theme Park Easter Pooh

Released March 1998.

Description This limited edition Pooh has a white pompon for a tail, and the ears on his head are held on by a scarf.

Availability Just like the other Easter Pooh, he's a hard one to locate.

Value History Gradually, he's risen to as much as $35.

Classic Pooh

Released December 1997.
Description Classic version of a classic.
Availability Disney Stores have plenty of Poohs.
Value History Unchanged.

Valentine Pooh

Released January 1998.

Description Pooh's limited Valentine edition wears a bumble bee outfit with red heart wings and red hearts on his antennae.

Availability Better ante up for this one.

Value History Pooh quickly sold out and values rose rapidly. Expect to pay at least $85.

Graduation/Grad Nite Pooh

Released May 1998.

Description Both versions of this limited edition toy wear cap and gowns, but the Walt Disney World Pooh sports Bermuda shorts under the gown.

Availability Look to the secondary market for Grad Nite Pooh and expect to buy with Mickey Mouse as part of a Grad Nite set.

Value History After a gradual increase, Pooh and Mick are worth about $45 as a set.

DISNEY SECTION

Pumbaa

Released January 1998.

Description Wisecracking sidekick of Simba in The Lion King.

Availability A Disney Store and Walt Disney World regular.

Value History Unchanged.

Rabbit

Released February 1998.

Description The cantankerous friend of Winnie the Pooh.

Availability Easy to find at Disney Stores and theme parks.

Value History Unchanged.

Queen of Hearts

Released May 1998.

Description This queen, part of the Alice in Wonderland line, puts Alice on trial.

Availability Unavailable at press time but rumored to be returning to Disney Stores.

Value History Until Queen of Hearts returns to the stores, expect to pay about $25 for her or $125 for the complete Alice in Wonderland set.

DISNEY SECTION

222

RED CARD MAN

Released May 1998.

Description One of the card men soldiers of the Queen of Hearts in Alice in Wonderland.

Availability Hard to find currently but rumored to be coming back to Disney Stores.

Value History Selling with other Alice in Wonderland characters for about $25 apiece.

Sebastian

Released September 1997.

Retired December 1997.

Description Production of the red crab friend of Ariel in the movie The Little Mermaid was short-lived.

Availability Even though retired, this character is still available at many Disney Stores and the theme parks.

Value History Unchanged.

Simba

Released January 1998.

Description Male lion cub from The Lion King.

Availability Very easy to find at Disney Stores, Walt Disney World or in the catalog.

Value History Unchanged.

Seven Dwarfs

Released July 1997.

Retired June 1998.

Description Sleepy, Sneezy, Dopey, Bashful, Grumpy, Happy and Doc all hail from the movie Snow White.

Availability Some Disney Stores and theme parks still carry some or all of the dwarfs, but they are getting harder to locate.

Value History Unchanged to date.

$7.00

DISNEY SECTION

226

Suzy Mouse

Released April 1998.

Description Female friend of Gus and Jaq Mouse from the movie Cinderella.

Availability Can be found at Disney Stores.

Value History Unchanged.

Thumper

Released September 1997.

Retired June 11, 1998.

Description Bambi's young rabbit friend in the animated classic Bambi.

Availability Thumper is still available at the Ttheme parks and many Disney Stores.

Value History Although still available, retirement has doubled Thumper's current retail price on the secondary market.

Tigger

Released September 1997.

Description Orange striped, bouncy friend of Winnie the Pooh.

Availability He may be the orly one, but there's plenty to go around at Disney Stores and theme parks.

Value History Unchanged.

Christmas Tigger

Released October 1997.
Description This limited edition beanie is simple; Tigger wears only a green scarf.
Availability No longer found at theme parks, Tigger is getting harder to locate.
Value History His stock is gradually climbing.

Classic Tigger

Released December 1997
Description Tigger in a simple, yet classy version.
Availability On stock at all Disney Stores.
Value History Unchanged.

Timothy

Released January 1998.

Description Mouse friend of Dumbo from the movie Dumbo comes in a regular and theme park version.

Availability Originally released only in the catalog, Timothy is now available at Disney Stores and the theme parks. He's also being released as a special event piece with the purchase of the Walt Disney Classic's Collection Dumbo Ornament.

Value History The standing version of Timothy is unchanged; the sitting version is worth at least double the retail price.

Timon

Released January 1998.

Description The meerkat from The Lion King who was responsible for a rash of zoo meerkat exhibits around the country.

Availability No need to visit the zoo; Timon is at Disney Stores and Walt Disney World.

Value History Unchanged.

DISNEY SECTION

Tramp

Released December 1997.

Description Mutt who falls for a pedigree cocker spaniel (Lady) in the film Lady and the Tramp.

Availability You can find Tramp and the other Lady and the Tramp characters at Disney Stores.

Value History Unchanged.

Trusty

Released June 1998.

Description Bloodhound friend of Lady in Lady and the Tramp.

Availability Look no further than Disney Stores.

Value History Unchanged.

TWEEDLE DEE

Released May 1998.

Description One of the many characters released from Alice in Wonderland.

Availability Tweedle Dee is hard to find now, but check with Disney Stores before shelling out big bucks on the secondary market.

Value History If Tweedle Dee and friends don't return to the stores, they could continue to soar past their $25 price per toy.

TWEEDLE DUM

Released May 1998.

Description Teamed with Tweedle Dee in Alice in Wonderland.

Availability Same as Tweedle Dee — currently unavailable in Disney Stores.

Value History The eight Alice in Wonderland characters are selling for as much as $120 a set.

Vulture

Released April 1998.

Description Vulture character from the movie Song of the South.

Availability Only available from the theme parks.

Value History Unchanged.

WHITE RABBIT

Released May 1998.

Description Funny character from Alice in Wonderland.

Availability As with other characters from the same movie, White Rabbit is currently unavailable in Disney Stores.

Value History Collectors still are paying about $25 for White Rabbit. If he returns to stores, however, his price will drop.

WOODY

Released December 1997.

Description Cowboy character from the computer-animated marvel Toy Story.

Availability Woody, and all Toy Story characters are at Disney Stores.

Value History Unchanged.

DISNEY SECTION

Bonus beanies are those toys that have always been harder to get because they aren't available at the U.S. Disney Stores, through mail order from the theme parks or at either of the two Club Disney Locations. Since they weren't available to everyone, many collectors consider their collections complete without them. And if they can purchase these toys, they are a "bonus" for their collection.

Disney's Bonus Beanies

Hamm

Released Unknown.

Description The pink pig from the movie Toy Story is a Japanese exclusive, although a smaller version has been released to Disney Stores in the U.S.

Availability If you don't plan on flying to Japan (the country doesn't ship beanies to the U.S.), your only opportunity to find this pig is on the secondary market.

Value History Hamm's value began high, dropped as the secondary market supply grew greater and then dropped dramatically when the U.S. version of Hamm debuted.

Cast Member Mickey

Released February 1997.

Description This very special Mickey dons a Disney Store cast member outfit.

Availability The beanie was given as a gift to cast members by Disney in 1997 and never made available to the public. Cast members were instructed not to sell the beanies.

Value History These special beanies climbed fast on the secondary market, many selling for more than $500.

ANIMAL KINGDOM DINOSAURS

Released April 1998.

Description The three-dinosaur set, which includes T-Rex, Brontosaurus and Triceratops, was created to herald the opening of the New Animal Kingdom Theme Park at Walt Disney World.

Availability The dinosaurs are exclusive to the Animal Kingdom theme park and are not available through mail order. The original set included Mousekeytoy tags that had the Dino's name. A newer set has Walt Disney World tags and no name.

Value History The first set has the most value because of the named tags, but both sets are in demand since they cannot be ordered through the mail.

Clutch and Scoop

Released Unknown.

Description These two bears in Anaheim Angels baseball outfits come complete with wings and a halo. They are not technically Mini Bean Bag Plush but have been adopted by collectors regardless.

Availability Clutch and Scoop may still be available from the Anaheim Angels site on the Internet at www.angelsbaseball.com.

Value History Unchanged.

Euro Disney Dalmatians

Released Unknown.

Description These three small Dalmatian pups (Lucky, Rose and Penny) are smaller than the Dalmatians Lucky and Jewel that are available in U.S. Disney Stores.

Availability Disneyland Paris was out of stock, but the pups might return to the shelves.

Value History As the pups remain sold out, their value steadily increases.

DISNEY SECTION

238

European Exclusive Soccer Mickey

Released May 1998.

Description Mickey and Donald hold soccer balls in this set.

Availability Mickey and Donald were limited to a run of 3,000 and 2,000, respectively, and when word reached the States and Internet sites began touting them, all of England was wiped clean within a day.

Value History Value rose quickly and has been steadily rising since. Expect to pay at least $130 for the set.

Animal Kingdom Tree Frog

Released April 1998.

Retired May 1998 (discontinued).

Description This green plush tree frog was created to celebrate the grand opening of Disney's newest theme park The Animal Kingdom. He was not originally considered part of the Mini Bean Bag Plush collection.

Availability Not even The Animal Kingdom has this rare frog.

Value History The tree frog's value escalated when he was discontinued after only a month, possibly because his design was too close to that of another tree frog at Walt Disney World. Expect to pay $400 or more for this sought-after collectible.

DISNEY SECTION

DISNEY SECTION

Japanese Jester Mickey and Minnie

Released Unknown.

Description These are the mascots of Disneyland Japan. Their tags identify them as special 15th anniversary characters, making them Disney collectibles as well as beanie collectibles. They have even been adopted by MBBP collectors.

Availability The only place to purchase them is the secondary market.

Value History Since they're not available at retail to most collectors, Jester Mickey and Minnie sell for about $110.

Disney & Other Beanies Price Guide

What the Columns Mean

The HI column represents full retail selling prices. The LO column represents the lowest price one could expect to find with extensive shopping.

DS–Disney Stores, MT–Mousekeytoys, WDW–Walt Disney World

1997-98 Disney Bean Bags

Abu - WDW Tag	10.00	20.00
Alien - DS Tag	7.50	15.00
Alien - WDW Tag	6.00	12.00
Animal Kingdom Tree Frog	550.00	750.00
Ariel - Video Premium	10.00	20.00
Bagheera - DS Tag	7.50	15.00
Baloo - DS Tag	6.00	12.00
Baloo - WDW Tag	6.00	12.00
Bambi - DS Tag	7.50	15.00
Bashful - DS Tag	7.50	15.00
Ben Ali Gator - DS Tag	6.00	12.00
Black Card - DS Tag	7.50	15.00
Brer Bear - WDW Tag	10.00	18.00
Brer Fox - WDW Tag	10.00	18.00
Brer Rabbit - WDW Tag	10.00	18.00
Brer Vulture - WDW Tag	10.00	18.00
Brontosaurus - WDW Tag	10.00	25.00
Bumble Bee Pooh - DS Tag	10.00	20.00
Buzz - WDW Tag	10.00	20.00
Buzz w/knee pads DS Tag	12.00	20.00
Buzz w/o knee pads DS Tag	7.50	15.00
Captain Hook - DS Tag	7.50	15.00
Cheshire Cat - DS Tag	10.00	20.00
Chip - DS Tag	6.00	12.00
Christopher Robbin - DS Tag	10.00	20.00
Classic Eeyore - DS Tag	7.50	15.00
Classic Eeyore - WDW Tag	7.50	15.00
Classic Piglet - DS Tag	7.50	15.00
Classic Piglet - WDW Tag	9.00	18.00
Classic Pooh - DS Tag	7.50	15.00
Classic Pooh - WDW Tag	7.50	15.00
Classic Tigger - DS Tag	7.50	15.00
Classic Tigger - WDW Tag	9.00	18.00
Croc - DS Tag	7.50	15.00
Daisy - DS Tag	7.50	15.00
Daisy - MT Tag	9.00	18.00
Dale - DS Tag	6.00	12.00
Dalmatian Pups European	50.00	80.00
Dewey - DS Tag	15.00	30.00
Dewey - WDW Tag	10.00	20.00
Doc w/glasses - DS Tag	10.00	20.00
Doc w/glasses - WDW Tag	10.00	20.00
Doc w/o glasses - DS Tag	9.00	18.00
Donald Duck - DS Tag	7.50	15.00
Donald Duck - MT Tag	12.00	20.00
Dopey (Test)	9.00	18.00
Dopey - DS Tag	9.00	15.00
Dopey - WDW Tag	7.50	15.00
Duchess w/whiskers/hard nose, no Tag	15.00	30.00
Duchess w/whiskers/soft nose, DS Tag	10.00	20.00
Duchess w/o whiskers DS Tag	7.50	15.00

Item	Low	High
Dumbo w/feathers - WDW Tag	10.00	20.00
Dumbo w/o feathers - DS Tag	9.00	18.00
Easter Pooh - DS Tag Retired	40.00	70.00
Easter Pooh - MT Tag	40.00	70.00
Eeyore (Test)	12.50	25.00
Eeyore blue - MT Tag	10.00	20.00
Eeyore grey - WDW Tag	12.50	25.00
European Soccer Donald	110.00	125.00
Fairfolk - DS Tag	6.00	12.00
Fantasia Hippo - DS Tag	6.00	12.00
Figaro - DS Tag	7.50	15.00
Figaro - WDW Tag	7.50	15.00
Figment - WDW Tag	15.00	30.00
Flounder (Test) - DS Tag Retired	20.00	35.00
Flounder - DS Tag Retired	10.00	20.00
Flounder - WDW Tag Retired	10.00	20.00
Flounder European	25.00	40.00
Flower - DS Tag	7.50	15.00
Flubber - DS Tag Retired	25.00	50.00
Genie - WDW Tag	10.00	20.00
Geppetto - DS Tag	7.50	15.00
Giggling Flubber - DS Tag	60.00	100.00
Giggling Flubber - MT tag	20.00	40.00
Goofy (Test)	18.00	30.00
Goofy - DS Tag	9.00	18.00
Goofy - MT Tag	7.50	15.00
Graduation Mickey - WDW Tag	30.00	50.00
Graduation Pooh - WDW Tag	35.00	60.00
Grumpy (Test)	12.00	20.00
Grumpy - DS Tag	9.00	18.00
Grumpy - WDW Tag	9.00	18.00
Gurgi - DS Tag	6.00	12.00
Gus the mouse - DS Tag	7.50	15.00
Hamm Japan	30.00	50.00
Happy - DS Tag	9.00	18.00
Hen Wen - DS Tag	6.00	12.00
Herbie the Love Bug - DS Tag	12.50	25.00
Huey - DS Tag	15.00	30.00
Huey - WDW Tag	10.00	20.00
Hula Minnie - DS Tag	12.00	20.00
Iago - WDW Tag	7.50	15.00
Jaq the mouse - DS Tag	7.50	15.00
Jewel - DS Tag Retired	18.00	30.00
Jiminy Cricket - DS Tag	10.00	20.00
Jiminy Cricket - WDW Tag	10.00	20.00
Kanga - DS Tag	10.00	20.00
Kanga - WDW Tag	10.00	20.00
King Louie - DS Tag	7.50	15.00
King Louie - WDW Tag	7.50	15.00
Lady - DS Tag	7.50	15.00
Lady - WDW Tag	7.50	15.00
Lady Cluck - DS Tag	7.50	15.00
Liberty Minnie - DS Tag	7.50	15.00
Little John - DS Tag	7.50	15.00
Louie - DS Tag	15.00	30.00
Louie - WDW Tag	10.00	20.00
Lucky European	20.00	40.00
Mad Hatter - DS Tag	7.50	15.00
Maid Marion - DS Tag	7.50	15.00
Marie 1st Version DS Tag	10.00	20.00
Marie 2nd Version DS Tag	10.00	20.00
Merlin - Club Disney	20.00	40.00
Mickey Mouse (Test) DS Tag	40.00	80.00
Mickey Mouse 2nd version DS Tag	18.00	30.00
Mickey Mouse 3rd version No stuffing, DS Tag	7.50	15.00
Mickey Mouse Chinese New Year DST Tag, Retired	350.00	500.00

Mickey Mouse Cast Member	400.00	700.00
Mickey Mouse MKT Tag	7.50	15.00
Minnie Mouse (Test)	50.00	100.00
Minnie Mouse 2nd Version DS Tag	18.00	30.00
Minnie Mouse 3rd version DS Tag	7.50	15.00
Minnie Mouse Chinese New Year DST Tag, Retired	350.00	500.00
Minnie Mouse - MT Tag	7.50	15.00
Mr. Smee - DS Tag	7.50	15.00
Nala - DS Tag	7.50	15.00
Nala - WDW Tag	9.00	18.00
Nana - DS Tag	7.50	15.00
101 Dalmations (Test) DS Tag	30.00	50.00
101 Dalmations w/o foot pads, DS Tag	15.00	25.00
Owl - DS Tag	9.00	18.00
Pain - Video Premium	15.00	25.00
Panic - Video Premium	15.00	25.00
Patch European	40.00	60.00
Pegasus - DS Tag Retired	30.00	50.00
Pegasus - MT Tag Retired	25.00	40.00
Pegasus - WDW Tag Retired	30.00	45.00
Penny European	40.00	60.00
Peter Pan - DS Tag	7.50	15.00
Piglet (Test) - DS Tag	25.00	45.00
Piglet 2nd Version - DS Tag w/o foot pads	9.00	18.00
Pilot Mickey	7.50	15.00
Pilot Pooh - DS Tag	10.00	25.00
Pinocchio - DS Tag	7.50	15.00
Pluto (Test)	18.00	30.00
Pluto - MT tag	7.50	15.00
Pumbaa - DS Tag	7.50	15.00
Pumbaa - WDW Tag	10.00	20.00
Queen of Hearts - DS Tag	7.50	15.00
Red Card - DS Tag	7.50	15.00
Reindeer Eeyore - DS Tag Retired	15.00	30.00
Reindeer Pluto - MT Tag Retired	15.00	30.00
Rex - DS Tag	6.00	12.00
Robin Hood - DS Tag	6.00	12.00
Safari Pooh -	18.00	30.00
Safari Piglet -	10.00	20.00
Safari Tigger -	12.00	20.00
Santa Mickey - DS Tag Retired	10.00	20.00
Santa Minnie - DS Tag Retired	10.00	20.00
Santa Pooh - DS Tag Hard nose, Retired	20.00	35.00
Santa Pooh - DS Tag Soft nose, Retired	15.00	30.00
Santa Pooh - WDW Tag	20.00	35.00
Santa Pooh - MT Tag	15.00	30.00
Santa Tigger - MT Tag	20.00	35.00
Sebastian (Test) DS Tag Retired	18.00	30.00
Sebastian 2nd Version DS Tag Retired	7.50	15.00
Sebastian European	25.00	40.00
Sebastian w/seam - WDW tag Retired	12.50	25.00
Simba - DS Tag	7.50	15.00
Simba - WDW Tag	9.00	18.00
Simba European	25.00	40.00
Sleepy - DS Tag	7.50	15.00
Sleepy - WDW Tag	7.50	15.00
Sneezy - DS Tag	7.50	15.00
Sneezy - WDW Tag	7.50	15.00

OTHER BEANIES PRICE GUIDE

Sorcerer Mickey - DS Tag	7.50	15.00
Spirit of Mickey/Mickey - DS Tag Video Premium	10.00	18.00
Spirit of Mickey/Minnie - DS Tag Video Premium	10.00	18.00
Suzy - DS Tag	7.50	15.00
Thumper - DS Tag	7.50	15.00
Tigger (Test) - DS Tag	35.00	60.00
Tigger 2nd Version DS Tag	20.00	35.00
Tigger 3rd Version DS Tag	10.00	20.00
Tigger 3rd Version WDW Tag	15.00	30.00
Timon - DS Tag	7.50	15.00
Timon - WDW Tag	9.00	18.00
Timothy Q - DS Tag	15.00	25.00
Toga Mickey - DS Tag	6.00	12.00
Tramp 8" - Brown collar DS Tag	12.50	25.00
Tramp 7" - Brown collar DS Tag	9.00	18.00
Tramp 7" - Rust collar DS Tag	7.50	15.00
Triceratops - WDW Tag	12.50	25.00
Tweedle Dee - DS Tag	7.50	15.00
Tweedle Dum - DS Tag	7.50	15.00
Tyrannosaurus Rex - WDW	12.50	25.00
Valentine Mickey - DS Tag Retired	10.00	20.00
Valentine Minnie - DS Tag Retired	10.00	20.00
Valentine Pooh - DS Tag Retired	75.00	125.00
White Rabbit - DS Tag	9.00	18.00
Winnie the Pooh (Test) w/footpads DS Tag	40.00	75.00
Winnie the Pooh 2nd version Soft nose/ w/o foot pads DS Tag	12.50	25.00
Winnie the Pooh 3rd version Hard nose DS Tag	7.50	15.00
Winnie the Pooh European	30.00	60.00
Woody - DS Tag w/buttons	12.50	25.00
Woody - DS Tag w/o buttons	6.00	12.00

1997-98 McDonald's Teenie Beanies

COMPLETE 1997 SET (10)	150.00	200.00
COMPLETE 1998 SET (12)	50.00	80.00
BAGGED PIECES PRICED BELOW UNBAGGED PIECES VALUED AT 50%		
Bones the dog	4.00	8.00
Bongo the monkey	9.00	15.00
Chocolate the moose	20.00	30.00
Chops the lamb	25.00	40.00
Doby the doberman	8.00	12.00
Goldie the goldfish	12.50	25.00
Happy the hippo	5.00	8.00
Inch the worm	5.00	8.00
Lizzy the lizard	10.00	20.00
Mel the koala	4.00	8.00
Patti the platypus	25.00	40.00
Peanut the elephant	5.00	8.00
Pinchers the lobster	4.00	8.00
Pinky the flamingo	30.00	50.00
Quacks the duck	10.00	20.00
Scoop the pelican	5.00	8.00
Seamore the seal	15.00	25.00
Snort the bull	10.00	20.00
Speedy the turtle	15.00	25.00
Twigs the giraffe	9.00	15.00

OTHER BEANIES PRICE GUIDE

246

1997 Nintendo Bean Bags

Bowser . . . . 3.00 . . . . . 6.00

Donkey Kong . . . . 3.00 . . . . . 6.00

Mario . . . . 3.00 . . . . . 6.00

Yoshi . . . . 3.00 . . . . . 6.00

1997-98 Puffkins

Albert the alligator . . . . 5.00 . . . . . 8.00
Born 2/8/98

Amber the tan monkey . . . . . 5.00 . . . . . 8.00
Born 7/31/97

Armour the armadillo . . . . . . 15.00 . . . . 30.00
Born 2/11/98
Retired

Aussie the koala . . . . 5.00 . . . . . 8.00
Born 5/17/97

Baldwin the eagle . . . . 5.00 . . . . . 8.00
Born 4/17/98

Bandit the raccoon . . . . 5.00 . . . . . 8.00
Born 2/21/97

Benny the black bear . . . . . . 5.00 . . . . . 8.00
Born 1/25/97

Biff the buffalo . . . . 5.00 . . . . . 8.00
Born 7/1/97

Bosley the bulldog . . . . 5.00 . . . . . 8.00
Born 3/9/98

Bruno the bull . . . . 6.00 . . . . 12.00
Born 2/17/98

Casey the cardinal . . . . 5.00 . . . . . 8.00
Born 3/23/98

Chomper the beaver . . . . 5.00 . . . . . 8.00
Born 2/5/97

Cinder the dalmation . . . . . . 5.00 . . . . . 8.00
Born 6/30/97

Cinnamon the tan cat . . . . . . 5.00 . . . . . 8.00
Born 9/21/97

Crystal the white bear . . . . . . 5.00 . . . . . 8.00
Born 3/19/98

Dinky the yel.dinosaur . . . . . . 7.50 . . . . 15.00
Born 9/9/97
Retired

Dottie the ladybug . . . . 5.00 . . . . 10.00
Born 2/19/98

Drake the red dinosaur . . . . . 7.50 . . . . 15.00
Born 8/21/97
Retired

Elly the elephant . . . . 5.00 . . . . . 8.00
Born 1/19/97

Fetch the brown dog . . . . 5.00 . . . . . 8.00
Born 4/7/97

Fetch the brown dog . . . . 7.50 . . . . 15.00
w/light brown nose

Flo the flamingo . . . . 5.00 . . . . . 8.00
Born 1/17/98

Franklin the red fox . . . . 5.00 . . . . 10.00
Born 1/31/98

Ginger the giraffe . . . . 5.00 . . . . . 8.00
Born 12/29/97

Grizwald the brn bear . . . . . . 5.00 . . . . . 8.00
Born 3/11/98

Gus the moose . . . . 5.00 . . . . . 8.00
Born 1/10/97

Henrietta the hippo . . . . 5.00 . . . . . 8.00
Born 7/21/97

Honey the tan bear . . . . 5.00 . . . . . 8.00
Born 3/27/97

Lancaster the lion . . . . 5.00 . . . . . 8.00
Born 2/27/97

Lily the frog . . . . 5.00 . . . . . 8.00
Born 2/28/97

Lily the frog . . . . 35.00 . . . . 60.00
Born leap year 2/29/97

Lilly the frog . . . . 20.00 . . . . 35.00
w/bright green feet

Lizzy the lamb . . . . 5.00 . . . . . 8.00
Born 10/6/97

Lucky the wh.rabbit . . . . 5.00 . . . . . 8.00
Born 4/23/97

Magic the unicorn . . . . 6.00 . . . . 12.00
Born 1/9/98

Max the gorilla	5.00	8.00
Born 1/1/97		
Meadow the cow	5.00	8.00
Born 3/13/97		
Milo the blk.monkey	5.00	8.00
Born 8/4/97		
Murphy the mouse	5.00	8.00
Born 5/1/97		
Nutty the squirrel	5.00	8.00
Born 5/22/97		
Odie the skunk	5.00	8.00
Born 12/9/97		
Olley the owl	5.00	8.00
Born 7/7/97		
Paws the wh.cat	5.00	8.00
Born 6/1/97		
Percy the pig	5.00	10.00
Born 4/18/97		
Peter the panda	5.00	8.00
Born 3/2/97		
Pickles the gr.dinosaur	7.50	15.00
Born 8/17/97		
Retired		
Quackster the duck	5.00	8.00
Born 5/2/97		
Shadow the blk.cat	5.00	8.00
Born 9/4/97		
Shelly the turtle	5.00	8.00
Born 2/12/97		
Shelly the turtle w/bright green feet	25.00	40.00
Slick the seal	5.00	8.00
Born 8/9/97		
Snowball the wh.tiger	75.00	150.00
Born 3/5/97		
w/black nose		
Retired		
Snowball the wh.tiger w/lavendar nose Retired	35.00	60.00
Snowball the wh.tiger w/pink nose Retired	35.00	60.00
Sound Flubber	15.00	30.00
Spike the porcupine	5.00	8.00
Born 1/28/98		
Tasha the white tiger	6.00	12.00
Born 11/7/97		
Tibbs the tan rabbit	5.00	8.00
Born 10/21/97		
Tiki the toucan	5.00	8.00
Born 3/30/98		
Tipper the tiger	5.00	8.00
Born 4/15/97		
Toby the whale	6.00	12.00
Born 10/11/97		
Retired		
Tomorrow Land Donald	7.50	15.00
Tomorrow Land Goofy	7.50	15.00
Tomorrow Land Mickey	7.50	15.00
Tomorrow Land Minnie	7.50	15.00
Tomorrow Land Pluto	7.50	15.00
Tourist Mickey	7.50	15.00
Trixy the wh.monkey	5.00	8.00
Born 6/20/97		
Tux the penguin	5.00	8.00
Born 6/12/97		
Zack the zebra	5.00	8.00
Born 11/26/97		

1997 Star Wars Buddies

Kenner		
Chewbacca w/black belt	6.00	12.00
Chewbacca w/brown belt	8.00	20.00
C-3PO	6.00	12.00
Jabba the Hutt	6.00	12.00
Jawa	6.00	12.00
Max Rebo	6.00	12.00
R2-D2	6.00	12.00
Salacious Crumb	6.00	12.00
Wicket	6.00	12.00

OTHER BEANIES PRICE GUIDE

OTHER BEANIES PRICE GUIDE

Waddle the penguin . . . . 5.00 . . . . . 8.00
Zip the cat . . . . 6.00 . . . . 10.00

1998 Coca-Cola Bean Bags

Coca-Cola can . . . . 7.50 . . . . 15.00
Penguin in Snowflake cap . . . . . 7.50 . . . . 15.00
Polar Bear in Driver's cap . . . . . 7.50 . . . . 15.00
Polar Bear in Plaid bow . . . . . . 7.50 . . . . 15.00
Polar Bear in Red Bow . . . . 7.50 . . . . 15.00
Polar Bear in Snowflake cap . . . 7.50 . . . . 15.00
Polar Bear in sweater . . . . 7.50 . . . . 15.00
Reindeer in shirt . . . . 7.50 . . . . 15.00
Seal in scarf . . . . 7.50 . . . . 15.00
Seal in skicap . . . . 7.50 . . . . 15.00
Seal in snowflake cap . . . . 7.50 . . . . 15.00
Walrus with can & scarf . . . . . 7.50 . . . . 15.00

1998 Grateful Dead Bean Bears

COMPLETE SET (11) . . . . 75.00 . . . 150.00
Althea . . . . 6.00 . . . . 15.00
Retired
Bertha . . . . 6.00 . . . . 15.00
Cassidy . . . . 6.00 . . . . 15.00
Cosmic Charlie . . . . 6.00 . . . . 15.00
Delilah . . . . 6.00 . . . . 15.00
Retired
Delilah w/o bl. Paws . . . . 8.00 . . . . 20.00
Retired
Jack Straw . . . . 6.00 . . . . 15.00
Retired
Samson . . . . 6.00 . . . . 15.00
St. Stephen . . . . 6.00 . . . . 15.00
Stagger Lee . . . . 6.00 . . . . 15.00
Sugaree . . . . 8.00 . . . . 20.00
Retired

Tennessee Jed . . . . 6.00 . . . . 15.00
Retired

1998 Harley Davidson Bean Bags

Big Twin bear . . . . 6.00 . . . . 12.00
Motorhead bear . . . . 6.00 . . . . 12.00
Punky pig . . . . 6.00 . . . . 12.00
Racer pig . . . . 6.00 . . . . 12.00
Ratchet pig . . . . 6.00 . . . . 12.00
Roamer bear . . . . 6.00 . . . . 12.00

1997 Meanies Bean Bags

COMPLETE SET . . . .
Armydillo Dan . . . . 6.00 . . . . 12.00
Terminated
Bart the Elephart . . . . 6.00 . . . . 12.00
Terminated
Boris the Mucousaurus . . . . . . 6.00 . . . . 12.00
Fi and Do the Dalmutation . . . . 6.00 . . . . 12.00
Hurly the Pukin' Toucan . . . . . 6.00 . . . . 12.00
Lucky the Rabbit - 1/2 Tag . . . 15.00 . . . . 35.00
Matt the Fat Bat . . . . 6.00 . . . . 12.00
Terminated
Navy Seal . . . . 6.00 . . . . 12.00
Terminated
Otis the Octopunk . . . . 6.00 . . . . 12.00
Terminated
Peter Gotta Peegull . . . . 6.00 . . . . 12.00
Sledge the HH Shark . . . . 6.00 . . . . 12.00
Terminated
Snake Eyes Jake . . . . 6.00 . . . . 12.00
Terminated
Splat the Road Kill Kat . . . . . . 8.00 . . . . 15.00

MARKET TRENDS

By Kathy Anderson

My advice has always been that if you're going to collect plush toys, even those market-savvy Beanie Babies, do it for fun and not the money. But if you're dead set on collecting beanies as an investment, the trend right now is to search for the newer releases.

It never ceases to amaze me why people are so desperate to get the new Beanie Babies as soon as they are released — and are paying huge amounts of money. I always think, "Why don't they relax and find them later when they're plentiful?"

But then I remember that Ty often does this ditty where they come out with a beanie and then think, "Why don't we change it?" The changed beanie hits the shelves a couple of months later and then the original beanie suddenly becomes more valuable.

So if you can't afford the older, retired ones, it makes sense to pursue new ones in the hope you're fortunate enough to find the original oddball release.

Pursuing new beanies also makes sense for those releases that have tag or name errors, or for those beanies which just never appear to reach the quantities of others.

For example, in the spring of 1997, Ty's Seamore was a tough find. It was clear from the network of collectors and dealers searching for him that he wasn't as abundant as his fellow Beanie Babies shipped at the same time. And, naturally, since there were no subsequent shipments of him after retirement, Seamore's price started to climb.

But before you decide to chase every scarce new release on the market, consider the possible consequences. The Princess bear, for example, was released in limited quantities in 1997 so that every store had a chance to receive it before the new year. On the secondary market, these bears were seen with price tags as high as $700. But as more stores received their shipments, the secondary market price began to drop, falling to about $100 by the following summer.

CONTRIBUTORS

KATHY ANDERSON

Kathy contributed information for the section on Ty Beanie Babies, as well as let us photograph her complete collection of beanies. Anderson has been collecting dolls for 25 years and designing dolls for Ashton Drake Galleries since 1987. She opened her shop, Maggie's Toy Box, in 1995 and has been a seller of all types of beanies and plush ever since. She has written for *Beckett Hot Toys* and Collecting Figures magazines. She is married and has five children: Maureen, Sara, Maggie and twins Katie and Matthew. In addition to plush animals, Anderson also collects the real thing. Her large home in the Chicago suburb of Des Plaines, Ill., is stocked with six retired research monkeys (Annie, Ben, Jessica, Emily, Timmy and Ginger), four cats, a dog, an iguana and an aquarium full of fish.

DUSTIE MEADS

Dustie wrote the section on Disney Plush and was brave enough to mail us about half of the Mini Bean Bags pictured in the Disney section. Meads publishes the on-line Disney Beanie Report and maintains the Web site www.dizbeanies.com, which received more than 350,000 hits in its first seven months. The Web designer and freelance writer also has contributed articles about Disney Mini Bean Bag Plush to *Beckett Hot Toys*, the Rosie Wells Beanie Gazette and Beans magazines. A resident of Joplin, Mo., Dustie is married and has one daughter.

PHYLLIS HOLLINSHEAD

We owe a hearty thanks to Phyllis, who contributed information for the Ty section. An assistant principal at an elementary school in Denton, Texas, Phyllis has been hotly pursuing plush collectibles for more than two years. Although her Ty collection numbers more than 100, her favorite beanie remains her first — Cubbie, purchased in 1994. A resident of Denton, Phyllis is married and has one son, also a beanie collector.

Our deepest appreciation also goes out to several contributors of items pictured throughout the book. They are Ty Inc. and Becketteers Mike Payne, Missy Patrello and Teri McGarey.

Similar fates, although to a lesser extent, awaited many Disney characters such as Christopher Robin and Dumbo. These Disney Mini Bean Bag Plush surged in value because of their initial scarcity. But once more of the plush were produced, the prices quickly dropped.

Meanwhile, retired beanies are at a standstill, possibly rising extremely high in value before leveling off in 1998. So I wouldn't put my eggs all in one basket by banking on the more expensive retired pieces to take off again in the near future.

I think beanies will always hold a value. I don't think they'll ever drop in value like, for instance, the Cabbage Patch Kids. (More than 80 million of the kids were "adopted," but Cabbage Patch dolls which once sold for hundreds of dollars on the secondary market are now being procured for about $40.) I've been in the collectibles field for 25 years and in all my days I've never, ever seen anything like this. I couldn't give you a comparison. It's just nuts.

People will say the phenomenon is like the Cabbage Patch dolls or the Power Rangers action figures, but it's not. Beanies have opened up opportunities for a slew of smaller accessory companies that are doing quite well. Entrepreneurs now design tag protectors, display cases, special beanie outfits, etc. And I know many hobby shops that would be in dire straits now were it not for beanies. You also can find plenty of plush at stores that once were exclusively sports card shops.

That's the good side to the boom. Beanies also appeal to all ages and sexes. Just the other day a 39-year-old man walked into my store under the pretense of buying a Glory bear for his 8-year-old daughter. He claimed he was a Harley-Davidson collector — and I don't mean the HD plush — but he soon gave himself away by explaining how Glory was just as much a symbol of Americana to him as any Harley he owned.

Certainly the Internet has played a role in the continued success of beanies. How much, I'm not quite sure. But once Ty created its Web sight (www.ty.com) in 1997, beanie collecting reached a frenzy pitch in the U.S. and suddenly branched out to Canada.

Ty's Web sight has generated an incredible amount of hits (1,832,922,360 through July 15th, 1998), rivaling McDonald's hamburgers sold — and they've been in business since 1952!

So I know Mr. Warner is attracting people on the Internet just so they can see what his site is going to display next. You can't argue with Ty's original formula: Keep 'em small, not mass produced, and sell 'em for a great price while making them hard to find.

Still, I can't completely figure out the mass appeal. I'm still saying, "Huh?" Yet, like everyone else, I'm still sucked into the craze.

MARKET TRENDS